NATURAL WAKEFULNESS

NATURAL WAKEFULNESS

*Discovering the Wisdom
We Were Born With*

Gaylon Ferguson

Foreword by Sakyong Mipham

Shambhala
Boston & London
2009

Shambhala Publications, Inc.
Horticultural Hall
300 Massachusetts Avenue
Boston, Massachusetts 02115
www.shambhala.com

© 2009 by Gaylon Ferguson

9 8 7 6 5 4 3 2 1

First edition
Printed in the United States of America

♾ This edition is printed on acid-free paper that meets the
American National Standards Institute z39.48 Standard.
♻ This book was printed on 30% postconsumer recycled paper.
For more information please visit us at www.shambhala.com.

Distributed in the United States by Random House, Inc.,
and in Canada by Random House of Canada Ltd

Interior design and composition: Greta D. Sibley & Associates

Library of Congress Cataloging-in-Publication Data

Ferguson, Gaylon Jules.
Natural wakefulness: discovering the wisdom we were born with /
Gaylon Ferguson; foreword by Sakyong Mipham.—1st ed.
p.   cm.
Includes bibliographical references and index.
ISBN 978-1-59030-657-4 (hardcover: alk. paper)
1. Meditation—Buddhism. 2. Spiritual life—Buddhism.
3. Awareness—Religious aspects—Buddhism. I. Title.
BQ5612.F47 2009
294.3'4435—DC22
2008037824

For my teachers:

Vidyadhara Chögyam Trungpa Rinpoche,
Sakyong Mipham Rinpoche—

Although we stumble,
we still aspire to see your face.

CONTENTS

Contents

FOREWORD

I LOVE MEDITATION, and clearly Gaylon Ferguson shares this love. Through his humble and brilliant insight, *Natural Wakefulness* reveals the unique relationship of meditation to the all-encompassing materialism we find ourselves in today. Based upon the Buddha's wisdom, this book lays out the clear and precise path of meditation as a valid and practical antidote to materialism in its many manifestations, not just simply as it pertains to consumerism, but also as it pertains to our inner being.

The Buddha stated that we are perfect and enlightened in every way. Our disbelief of this reality produces a level of insecurity that makes us clamor for both psychological and physical objects as a way to feel whole and complete. The path of meditation helps us regain our trust in the inner brilliance that the Buddha mentioned so long ago. Without such a tool by which to handle the mind, it goes on a conceptual rampage, devouring the past, present, and future. As a result we feel numb to the world's problems, or overwhelmed by them.

For years I have encouraged Gaylon to write his unique insights, which I am delighted can be shared with the rest of you. No doubt my father, Chögyam Trungpa Rinpoche, would be as delighted as I am at Gaylon's humor, humility, and vision. The advice in this book will be of tremendous benefit to those who have the courage to engage their mind and heart and develop their potential. As a result, it will benefit the greater world.

The Sakyong, Jamgön Mipham Rinpoche
Halifax, Nova Scotia, 2008

INTRODUCTION

THIS BOOK ENCOURAGES SPIRITUAL AWAKENING. Initially I called it "waking up from the nightmare of materialism." The approach presented here begins with wakefulness as our original, basic state of being alive. The journey of meditation practice follows as a natural unfolding of this innate awareness and kindness. The result of walking the spiritual path is experiencing the openness and warmth of life in community. These are the three main sections of the book: (1) contemplating wakefulness and sleep, (2) the practice of meditation as a way of uncovering our original nature, and (3) gathering with others as the expression of wakeful compassion. It seemed particularly important, given that we live in a time of such pervasive fear and doubt about each other's fundamental goodness, to end by reflecting on the essential importance of establishing sane communities. Dr. King called this the "dream of beloved community."

Before you take the journey through what's written here, let me say something about how I came to write this. I entered the path outlined here in the early 1970s at Tail of the Tiger Buddhist meditation center in northern Vermont. There, following some summer seminars in *buddhadharma,* I received instruction in sitting practice from the Tibetan meditation master Chögyam Trungpa Rinpoche. I do not recall the words he used to convey the meditative state, but the atmosphere I experienced while sitting with him was vivid and seemed the essence of the communication.

Following some years of practice—including in particular several month-long meditation retreats—I began leading group meditation retreats in the mid-1970s at the suggestion of my teacher. I was still a relatively inexperienced meditation instructor, having taught just two courses in mindfulness and insight, both at the recently formed Naropa Institute (later to become Naropa University). The first group retreat I led was a small (perhaps twenty participants) monthlong program in northern California. When the retreat's coleader informed me that she needed to leave for an important weekend with our teacher in Boulder, Colorado, I greeted this news with much late-night pacing, worrying, and general anxiety about the well-being of the fledgling meditators temporarily left in my care. I was not quite twenty-four.

The month passed uneventfully—one night a bat got into a participant's room, and we gently coaxed it back outside. In the long hot days of sitting, there were several earnest requests for midday treks to a local river. We persevered, rising near dawn for sitting and walking, and then sitting and walking again and again until nine or so every evening. The mostly vegetarian food we all helped prepare was decent, and the overall spiritual companionship of the group was supportive and encouraging.

I do not recall anyone's attaining enlightenment—or even any of the temporary experiences of satori and *kensho* I had read about years earlier as an impressionable teenager poring over *The Three Pillars of Zen* and the writings of D. T. Suzuki in my messy college dorm room. Over the course of the month I gave several nervous, stammering talks on the relationship of awakened nature and meditation practice, and I met one-to-one with each of the participants. Amid the meandering recounting of stories of previous engagements with other spiritual practices and encounters with various swamis, *roshis,* lamas, druids, Gurdjieff teachers, and Krishnamurti (this was, after all, not that far from the 1960s), I eventually noticed a theme.

All of us tended either to approach our meditation practice with much more exertion than was necessary (or helpful) or, tiring ourselves out from a day of gung ho sitting, to lapse into looseness. Basically, we were either trying too hard or not making enough effort. I remembered the Buddha's early instruction on finding a "middle way" between excessive tightness and excessive looseness. As with learning a dance like the Argentine tango, this simple yet profound teaching is something one has to actually *do* to understand fully. Tightening and loosening are said to be skills used by even advanced meditators practicing *mahamudra* meditation.

Eventually a key connection dawned: tightening and loosening are directly related to joining nature and training, two important principles along the path. There is the need for both trust in our innate wakefulness and confidence in the path to uncovering that nature. When we are excessively tight, vigilantly on guard, there is not enough appreciation of our fundamentally awake nature. Right meditation is not a matter of successfully manipulating our experience. Practicing with relaxed appreciation of basic wakefulness can become a part of living a life of nonaggression. On the other hand, if—hearing the message of original goodness— we confidently lapse into daydream upon daydream, then clearly there is not enough application of discipline and exertion. The teachings in this book are based on appreciating original nature while training in meditation.

Beginning with a three-month intensive training program in 1999, I received a second wave of classic instructions in the practice of Buddhist meditation, this time from Trungpa Rinpoche's lineage heir and eldest son, Sakyong Mipham Rinpoche. In the dozens of weekend, weeklong, and month-long group meditation retreats I have taught over the last decade, the dharma streams of these two teachers have merged into one river of instruction. *Natural Wakefulness* is dedicated to these two meditation masters, holders of the treasury of oral instructions of the Practice Lineage, because they are the source of the meditation teachings in this book and in the group retreats it is based on. If there are mistakes in transmitting this pure gold, the fault is solely my own.

A NOTE ON THE BOOK'S FORMAT

Natural Wakefulness contains, alongside teachings about this particular approach to the spiritual path, a sequence of guided contemplations and meditation exercises. At the back of the book, there are notes giving the sources for most quotations, as well as explanations of some key terms. Occasionally there are also dialogues—question-and-answer exchanges—with comments and insights from many meditators practicing these instructions in group retreats. The questioning voices in these dialogues appear like this:

Question: If we're all naturally awake, why do we need to train in meditating?

These exchanges are essential to the experience of reading this book. They display and celebrate the interweaving of confusion and insight that is the experience of walking the path for many of us. Your own questions and discoveries while reading and meditating become an important part of this shared unfolding of basic wisdom. Welcome to the twenty-five-hundred-year-old conversation!

NATURAL WAKEFULNESS

1 Awakening to the Life of Reruns

LET'S BEGIN WITH NATURAL WAKEFULNESS and its connection with the path of meditation. In meditation retreats over the years, I've been asked many times: "Why is it natural to 'wake up'?" After some conversation among the group, circling around the deeper meaning of "awake" as our natural state of being, someone will occasionally grow bolder still and raise a hand to wonder out loud: "If it's so natural, why do I need to meditate?"

Meditation is the natural path of spiritual awakening. The Buddha discovered a "middle way" of developing our innate human potential, an approach to meditating that avoids the twin traps of trying to force the mind to be still or letting it run wild. Right meditation skillfully joins our basic awakened nature with the practice of gently training the mind and heart.

The word "buddha" means "awakened one." Imagine that one day, walking among the fresh vegetables of your local farmer's market, you suddenly see someone with unusual presence—calm, compassionate, clear. What are the signs of this? It might be the graceful way the person moves: body and mind in easy harmony with each other. It might be the person's gentle tone of voice, the friendly way of speaking to the checkout person. It might just be the bright clarity and steady kindness of the gaze; the eyes can be the windows of wakefulness.

Seeing such a person, we might wonder: Who is this? Where did this wise person come from? How is it that someone could be radiating such peace and sanity in the midst of so much anxiety, aggression, and speed? The most important question we might ask ourselves is: how did this person get to be this way? As soon as we begin to contemplate awakening, wondering about it—where it comes from, how to get there—we are already on the path to enlightenment. Our curiosity is a sign of inner wakefulness uncoiling itself.

The Buddha's powerful yet gentle presence inspired many similar questions among those he met: "What are you? Are you a supernatural being? Is there a way for us to become more at peace with life, more grounded and open—the way you are? What should we call you?" Smiling, he answered: "I am awake, so you should call me, 'Awakened One'—and here is a noble path to your own awakening."

This name, "Awakened One," is an answer—but also a question: Awakened from what? Awake to what? Clearly the famous "awakened state of being" involves more than just rising with a yawn and a few stretches from an ordinary night of restful sleep to face the challenges of another day. We are concerned here with deeper senses of "asleep" and "awake." We are beginning the journey to complete realization by contemplating the meaning of enlightened wakefulness and spiritual sleep.

The first step of true awakening involves realizing our habitual, everyday, walk-around state of being "asleep." Our distracted, daydream-filled life has been compared to sleep-walking. As we know, sleepwalkers often dream on in relative comfort—until they suddenly bump into a wall or step off a staircase. The resulting "ouch!" experience corresponds to the discovery of what the Awakened One called "the noble truth of suffering."

Certainly the Buddha's own spiritual path involved first waking up to his sleepwalking state. Suddenly—with a penetrating glimpse of the painful realities of human life outside the cozy comfort of his parents' palace, he saw that he had been living in a pleasant dream. The bubble of indulgent life at court was a seductive trap, lulling him into a false sense of security, keeping him from seeing the bright truth of real life. For Prince Siddhartha, recognizing confusion was the crucial first step on the way to enlightenment, a milestone in his journey to complete freedom from confused suffering.

This is the victory cry of the unbroken lineage of awakened ones: there is a path that leads to liberation. We can free ourselves from the automatic, habitual thoughts and emotions that so often bind us into familiar psychological prisons. The good news is that liberation is possible. Our first major challenge is facing the trap of self-imprisonment, for the path to true freedom begins with insight into our routines of self-deception. Our initial awakening is to the sleep state, our lack of self-awareness.

When I moved from the San Francisco Bay area to Seattle for a new job, one of the first things I noticed was how many attitudes and feelings I carried over from the old workplace. Like a turtle with its personal, conveniently portable shell, I transported my own little mental environment around with me all the time, from one city to another. Monday morning I might be introduced to a new employee, Jay, just hired, someone I'd never met before. By Wednesday, having talked some with Jay in the elevator and at the copy machine, he's beginning to remind me of Tim, my supervisor at a previous job. I'm not really sure what it is about Jay—the way he jumps right in to finish my sentences for me (just the way Tim did)? The way he seems so quick to boast about himself and his impressive family background? (Tim also tended toward arrogance.) Soon—by the Friday afternoon office party—and before I even realize it, I am relating to Jay (swerving toward avoidance) mainly based on my irritating past experiences with Tim.

One day, chatting in a way that I later recognized as cruising along on automatic pilot, I begin complaining to one of my friends about this new guy at work, "Tim"—and then catch myself midsentence when I suddenly remember that there's no one in our department by that name! My thoughts, feelings, and actions in the present are largely based on what I'm carrying over from the past, the earlier work relationship. Sound familiar? This pattern appears again and again, at work and in love, both within the family and in business relationships.

This has very little to do with experience in the present. After all, I've only just met Jay, but already I recognize him as a certain type that I've had difficulties with in the past. Prompted by this experience of emotional hangover, I move through my day with a slightly heightened awareness of this recurrent pattern. Now I'm noticing example after example of this repeated framing of the present in the long-gone terms of the past. "Here it is again, just like last week's planning session. Jane is criticizing the whole team, so it's gonna be one of those meetings." "She reminds me of Karen, my old friend from college. They have the same wacky sense of humor. Probably we will get to be great friends." "Here comes another week of predictable hassles with Gerald about receipts and reimbursements." "I hope my boss likes my work on the new project as much as he did last quarter."

Clearly, most of my hopes and fears about the future are based on what went well—or badly—in the past. Yesterday, last week, the previous year, the last time we faced a similar challenge—the past seems to haunt the present like the ghosts that come back to taunt old Scrooge. Memories accumulate and spread like mold. Soon these mushrooming projections from the past entirely fill the space of the future.

The more I notice this sum of thoughts (mentally carried over from the past) shaping my reactions in the present, the more I feel the pinch of the sleepwalking state. That pinch is the awakening of insight. I've caught a glimpse of my internal cage, the tight, mental prison I drag along with me wherever I go. Living inside the turtle's shell no longer seems so cozy. Even if Jay turns out to be very different from Tim, I will probably mistake many of these differences as just more of the "same old, same old." I will miss a lot, perhaps most, of what's new and fresh in this moment.

This is humbling: the root of my dissatisfaction is not with others—my partner or the coworkers at my job or the new neighbors. One great Tibetan meditation teacher counseled that seeing bad qualities in others is like looking in the mirror and discovering the dirt on one's own face. Yet, as humbling as this glimpse of the truth of pervasive distraction and projection can be, it is an insight. I discover that I'm repeatedly tuning in to the replay of mental reruns from similar situations in the past. As a result, my perceptions, feelings, and reactions are often stale and hollow—like the canned laughter of an old television show. Insight lets us see that it's time to change channels—or turn off the TV entirely.

A PRIMARY DISCOVERY

Much of our present experience is based on reruns. Sudden passionate attachments and fixations (seemingly out of nowhere, the feeling of "gotta have it"), angry outbursts or festering resentments (still seething after all these years), viewing ourselves as dutifully plodding along (with the hum of a drone)—we've lived through similar scripts and emotional dramas before. We enlist any available innocent bystanders into the cast of the current play. Whether it's a soap opera or a sitcom, there's an ongoing, open casting call: "Hey! Would you like to play the part of . . . ?"

This is an essential discovery on the path of awakening: our experience of life and the world is strongly flavored by our own internal cycles of mental weather—sunny, foggy, rainy, sunny, misty, cloudy—and around and around we go: jealous, proud, anxious, craving, excited, deflated. When we look closely, we discover that we have deeply ingrained habits of distracting ourselves from the present. But with insight, we clearly see the mountainous challenge that looms large before us.

What is this mountain? The accumulated momentum of distraction piled upon distraction on top of distraction. It's like a giant car-crash pileup. Seeing the possibility of continuing to spin this slippery web of mindlessness of the present, we are inspired to plant both feet firmly on the meditation path of nowness. Insight into our mental prison sparks the motivation for walking the path.

For a while, we think, maybe this is so; maybe it is this way at least sometimes. But we waver. Our momentary glimpse of certainty in the truth of suffering becomes uncertain. Over time, we slide back into habits of emotional reaction and justification: "It's right that I feel this way: Tim, I mean Jay, *is* a jerk!" We gradually move toward establishing a more comfortable nest in the prison—perhaps in that newly remodeled wing with a nice view of the outside. We lose sight of the motivation for true freedom, for the cool spaciousness of liberation. We forget, until the feeling of being stuck in a stuffy trap without windows arises again.

HOW CAN I WAKE UP FROM SLEEPWALKING?

Even to ask such a question is to set out on the path of awakening. We value one-click-away answers a great deal in our hyperquick digital information age, but some of our questions are even more valuable. Holding off for a moment from superficial, quick-fix answers allows us to see that asking such questions is itself a golden thread linking our inquisitive intelligence to the treasury of innate wisdom. In his classic guide to the spiritual path, *Meditation in Action,* Chögyam Trungpa suggests that some questions contain their own answers: "The first stage . . . is to ask oneself, 'Who am I?' Though this is not really a question. In fact it is a statement, because 'who am I?' contains the answer."

To question is to ask, What would it mean to be an awake human being? What does a fully human life look like? What do I truly aspire to be? Contemplative questioning takes us into the depths of our experience beyond the superficiality of downloaded assumptions. All too frequently, our experience of the roller-coaster ride of mental ups and downs is taken as normal—as though the grasping and aggression of our sleepwalking are all that is natural to the human condition. We take for granted our mental imprisonment, as though everyone is tuned to the same blaring talk-radio station, WCAT: All Confusion, All the Time. Doesn't everyone feel this way?

Encountering an awakened person gives the lie to this conventional assumption. All of us have been inspired by the example of women and men living with confidence, loving-kindness, and dignity. Our questions about a path to freedom arise from an inner intuition that, at the very basis of our being, we share the same enlightened potential we admire in great, compassionate wisdom-beings. As the pathbreaking

Japanese Zen meditation master Suzuki Roshi taught: "It is wisdom which is seeking wisdom."

To proceed farther along the path, we need to turn awareness toward our present state of being. The title of the American Buddhist nun Pema Chödrön's *Start Where You Are* says it well. If we catch even a passing glimpse of our distractedness, even a whiff of our lost-in-thought, continually-daydreaming-about-the-past-and-future ordinary state, we've already begun to wake up. Ordinarily, we might take the discovery of the sleepwalking state as a setback—as though we took a step forward only to find ourselves stuck on a treadmill, walking in place, over and over. But rather than taking this discovery as a signal for discouragement, we can view this penetrating experience of our mental habits as the dawning of insight. Clearly seeing the bad news *is* good news. Waking up starts with noticing the rushing stream of distraction. It's like turning a corner and coming upon a buzzing, inner geyser.

The heart of the practice of meditation is to come back to the experience of our present state again and again. We start where we are, and then, when we wander, return to where we are, and then, if necessary, return again. We feel the restlessness of our internal dialogue, always wondering, What's next? What comes after this? What's beyond this busy, talking-to-myself-mind? Being caught up in the questions and movement of this speedy mind is distraction itself. Distraction feeds on the anxious feeling of wanting to be elsewhere, waiting for something else, something different to arrive. Instead, we are waking up by mindfully examining the habits and routines of the everyday sleepwalking state, following the meandering course of our inner river of memories and fantasies, the babbling brook of our almost constantly overlapping thoughts.

CHECKING IN WITH OUR EXPERIENCE

If we are at all unsure about the truth of distraction in our ordinary state of being, our everyday life, then let's pause for a moment to check, to see for ourselves how it actually is right now. It's crucially important that we test these teachings on wakefulness against the truth of our own experience. So, please put the book down for a moment, sit comfortably, and then just take notice of what is happening physically and mentally for you at this very moment. Take two or three minutes to notice and inquire in a curious and friendly way: What is happening with the body—notice the play of physical sensations, perceptions, feelings. What is happening in the mind? Any thoughts? Are these mostly thoughts about the future? Thoughts about the past? Any hopes or anxieties? A mixture of the two? Feelings of happiness? Sadness? Boredom? Excitement? Just notice your own state of being—body, mind, and heart, as you are right now. Are there just a few thoughts—like a tiny trickle from a faucet? Or is it more like a gushing waterfall, thoughts upon thoughts upon thoughts, one after another, rushing forward in a continuous stream? Look. Take note of what is happening, inquiring with loving-kindness. If you find your mind repeatedly drifting to last night's dinner conversation or next week's planning meeting, notice that—and instead of jumping into the details of the past (why did she say that?) or future (what will I do when I get there?), gently return to this focused inquiry into the present: what is happening in body and mind, right now? Look with gentle curiosity, and see what is actually happening.

As we are inquiring into our present state, doubtful, skeptical thoughts about the whole process may emerge: "I don't feel like I'm distracted by thoughts of the future or the past.

Many of my thoughts are about the present. Sure, I'd rather be doing something (anything) else right now. What's the point of this exercise, anyway? I don't think I'm sleepwalking through life, at least not most of the time. Has it been three minutes yet?" Again, the truth is not a matter of belief or accepting some traditional dogma. Truth is uncovered by closely examining our own experience. Answers are discovered through seeing what is actually happening in our body and mind. Here, the proof of the recipe is definitely found in the taste of the pudding. Cook—and then taste-test for yourself. Just look and see what is happening at present. Don't take anyone's word for it. Look—honestly and directly.

Just notice—and then notice again, noticing what's happening in the next moment and then the one after that.

DON'T REJECT ANYTHING

Even this simple exercise of precise awareness and honesty involves bravery—we're letting go of our preconceived ideas about what our experience is (or should be) and taking a fresh look for a change. We're letting go of old judgments. We're not trying to make anything in particular happen or achieve a specific state of mind. We're not meditating. We're just noticing what is already going on in the present—without any manipulation. Don't try to hold on to what occurs: If it feels relatively pleasant to sit simply for a moment like this, let it be that way. If it feels like nothing special is happening, then let that be as well. Similarly, if it feels slightly uncomfortable and unfamiliar, let that feeling of awkwardness arise. Does it linger and then dissipate? Above all, don't condemn or reject anything that's arising in your experience: "Is this really the way my mind jumps around all day long—like a grasshopper that's had too many espressos? That wasn't a very loving thought, now was it? Why am I still thinking about that? What comes next, what comes next, what comes next? Is this what's supposed to be happening? What's wrong with me today? I think I was more present last week—what happened?"

In Robert Heinlein's science-fiction novel *Stranger in a Strange Land,* he describes several truthful, even-handed beings called Fair Witnesses. Adopt the attitude of "fair witnessing" toward all your experience for a moment, gradually relaxing the pervasive compulsion to grasp and hug the best and happiest moments while avoiding the ugly, unpleasant ones. As much as possible, return again and again to noticing, noticing, just noticing, with a simple, nonjudgmental attitude of curiosity and gentle inquiry. What is happening here and now for you, within your own experience? Notice with the open attitude of a good friend you haven't seen for a while. This is the friend who genuinely wants to know your state of being, who asks and then listens carefully to hear the answer to the question: how are you? Listening in your own experience for the answer to this contemplative question is the essence of genuine self-reflection.

MORE THAN A FAIR-WEATHER FRIEND TO OURSELVES

In this simple way, we begin to make true friends with ourselves in a thorough and profound way instead of being a fair-weather friend. We say, "Jack and Jane are mostly fair-weather friends," meaning these are friends we can spend time with when all is going well and sailing along smoothly, but during high-stress times of grief and loss, illness, or divorce, Jack and Jane don't come around. The invitation of a daily meditation practice is to move beyond such a superficial, fair-weather friendship with ourselves.

After all, it's fairly easy to love those aspects of ourselves that others approve of, the facets of our personality we are rewarded or admired for. What about the less praiseworthy aspects of our being, our less savory emotional habits? Losing our temper over a minor hassle. Endlessly procrastinating. Pushing ahead in traffic without regard for the feelings and needs of others. Waffling back and forth with fearful, worried indecision. Covering over our moments of insecurity by faking it, blustering our way through any conflict or challenge, afraid to show our true feelings to anyone. Part of the power of genuine spiritual practice is that we sit in meditation with ourselves during all the seasons of our life, during the falls and winters of trouble and defeat no less than the springtimes and summers of victory and celebration.

This is the royal road to enlightenment, approaching meditation as a process of making friends with oneself. This is the path of meditation as loving-kindness practice—we begin by first extending gentleness and kindness to ourselves.

This noticing, this wakeful, caring interest in our present state of mind and body, is itself natural. Appreciative inquiry expresses our true nature. We all have an inborn, native sense of care for ourselves. Attention expresses respect. Awareness of our own state of being is the basis of self-respect. Awakening starts with appreciating this natural interest and then gradually expanding the appetite for self-knowledge. Self-knowledge is the vanguard of wisdom. We begin with this innate appetite for knowing, and we return to it again and again, going with the grain of our own deepest inclination. We want to go beyond the illusions of sleepwalking to wake up to ourselves as we truly are, so we inquire: what am I sensing, feeling, thinking now? This basic level of self-awareness and self-reflection is readily available to all of us. Self-knowledge is the essential ground for the entire spiritual path.

DIALOGUES ON MAKING FRIENDS WITH ONESELF AND COMPASSION

At this point, you may be wondering, "What's all this about caring for oneself? I thought that spirituality had to do with caring for and helping others. What about the famous connection between meditation and compassion?" Many participants from group meditation retreats have wondered out loud along similar lines, asking, "Isn't it kind of narcissistic to pay so much attention to myself? What about all the troubles in the world today? What about all the others who are suffering? How is this helping them?"

Compassion begins at home. The heart of loving-kindness is awakened through caring for ourselves, as well as those near to us, those we easily feel love and compassion for. Then we extend that same warmth and concern to others, who are more distant, less familiar. The more expansive the circle of our care, the more we discover the big heart of true compassion.

The key point is that this path of awakening the heart is a natural process—it's going with the grain of our own basic goodness, following the flowing movement of an instinctive desire to wake up. We already have a powerful appetite for wisdom. We long to rediscover our inborn strength—a mind filled with kindness. We are uncovering a spontaneous aspiration to find the courage whose closest ally is tenderness.

What is it that first inspired you to read a book about the path of meditation? Why are you interested in the topic of wakefulness at all? What is the source of this motivation and interest? To say that "it is wisdom which is seeking wisdom" is to affirm our inmost desire to wake up and be of benefit to others. We have a strong, natural appetite for the nourishing foods of wisdom and love. It is our fundamentally compassionate nature that is attracted to teachings on compassion. In the *I Ching* (the Chinese classic often translated as the *Book of Changes*), the image for this spontaneous inner resonance is one songbird calling to its mate, who answers because they are of the same nature. Similarly, we respond to the call of our own true nature, the heart of compassion.

If it were not so—if our own true nature were not already tending in this direction—we would be repelled by the very sound of the syllables "loving-kindness" or the word "compassion." Like insects avoiding the awful smell of bug repellent, we would stay as far away as possible from all mention of caring for others. "Ugh! Get out of here—I hate that kind of talk!" Instead we would seek out more teachings and practices for cultivating selfishness, indifference, and aggression. Consider the responses to the tragedies of the events of September 11 in 2001, the Indonesian tsunami in 2004, and the Gulf Coast hurricane Katrina in 2005. Many people around the world felt spontaneous upsurges of empathy for the suffering of others—and acted with corresponding generosity. Compassion is as natural to us as breathing, even if for many of us, tenderness and compassion have been temporarily covered by fear and doubt.

WHAT IS NATURAL WAKEFULNESS?

This book's title echoes similar phrases from the Buddhist tradition: original nature, fundamental wisdom, basic goodness. Are these different words for the same thing? Perhaps. What's more important than the menu is actually tasting the meal. We live in a time in which we doubt the fundamental trustworthiness of our experience. This has become so pervasive that we wonder if it isn't just as natural to be selfish and distracted as it is to be open and kind. To clarify this essential point, let's return to the main theme of this chapter: the relationship between natural wakefulness and meditating.

Our original nature is the single most important element on the path of waking up. Why? Because it is the essential ingredient—without the natural impulse to wake up, there cannot be a path of meditation or a spiritual journey at all. Practicing meditation without this original wisdom-nature would be like gardening all summer without any seeds—we could prepare the ground and water the soil, even pick away the weeds and insects, but without seeds, we know that nothing will grow. Similarly, no movement along the path is possible without this primary motive force. It would be like setting out to travel across town but not walking, running, biking, driving, or using any other means of transportation. How could we possibly move without motivation? True nature is our motive force.

Trungpa Rinpoche urged us to study the sayings of an ancient Indian Buddhist wisdom teacher named Tilopa. Tilopa—whose name means "sesame-seed person"—used the analogy of sesame seeds to point to the importance of our fundamental nature. Without the seeds we cannot obtain the inner essence, the sesame oil, the fruit of the meditative path. Even if we dutifully press sand or gravel for hours upon hours all day, every day for a month, we won't find any sesame oil. This simple analogy illuminates a profound truth: the spiritual path is not just a matter of effort and forceful will. Success on the path—what's sometimes called "realization"—is never the product of sheer exertion, of trying and trying to get there. "Realization" means realizing what is always already here in potential form. From the beginning, the oil is present in the seed; it simply needs pressing to draw it out.

The awakened state lies dormant, an ignored potential within us, but we need consistent training in meditation to awaken this sleeping giant. There is a saying in the traditional Buddhist teachings of Tibet: "The ultimate materialism is believing one has to manufacture the buddha-wisdom." All our grasping after unusual experiences or higher spiritual states comes from lack of confidence in the power of this original nature.

HOW DO I GAIN CONFIDENCE IN NATURAL WAKEFULNESS?

The analogy of the sesame seeds also illuminates the second most important aspect of the spiritual path—training. Here we are primarily exploring the topic of training in the discipline of the sitting practice of meditation. Training, cultivating—actually doing something to draw the inner essence out, to develop it—is absolutely necessary. Merely thinking about practice, intending to get to it someday soon, is not enough. As Tilopa explains: "If by the combination of mortar and pestle and hands, the beating and extraction are not done, one cannot obtain the oil." If we simply sit staring at the bowl of sesame seeds in front of us, wondering when the sesame oil will magically appear—nothing happens. It's not enough just to think, "Open sesame!" As it says in the genealogies of the biblical scriptures, nothing begets nothing. No pressing of the seeds, no sesame oil.

The seed of our awakened nature is an essential ingredient; it's absolutely necessary, but it's not sufficient by itself for awakening. If we don't apply our attention and fully engage body and mind, stagnation soon sets in. Sleepwalking continues to reign. The net result? We find ourselves repeating the same scenarios, living out the familiar routines of habit, again and again and again. The accumulated power of our ingrained distraction is so strong that it easily overrides our momentary good intentions, like floodwaters snuffing out a matchstick's flickering flame. We make a New Year's resolution not to lose our temper, but then two weeks into January we hear ourselves snapping at someone at home or at work. Facing a tough deadline, we catch ourselves cursing at a slow driver on the freeway.

So, just as the teaching of an originally wakeful nature tells us that the path is not a matter of just working at it, the complementary teaching of training—particularly training through the discipline of meditation practice—tells us that just trusting in the fundamental goodness of our original nature is also not enough. As we know, it's not enough merely to believe that exercise improves our well-being—actually getting to the gym or going out for a walk or a run is another, crucial matter. Similarly, it's not enough simply to have naive faith or belief in the goodness of our original nature.

WHY NOT?

Why isn't original goodness isn't enough? If we're naturally awake, why do we need to train?

Particularly at first, our trust and confidence in basic goodness are based largely on ideas and concepts. We have heard or read about inherent enlightened nature, and we say, "Yes—this makes some sense to me; it sounds good. Yes . . . yes, I think I believe in basic goodness." This is fine, to begin with—where else could we start except with a somewhat vague sense of belief, a slightly naive faith in this possibility? Again, we have to start where we are. Wisdom is already there in our initial inspiration.

However, remaining with just this vague outline—the "finger-painting level"—would be like skipping the meal and instead continuing to chew on the menu in a good restaurant. ("Hmm, this cardboard could use more salt.") Menus are helpful and often whet the appetite, but the point is to actually taste the tomato soup. Training in meditation corresponds to actual experience—smelling the aroma of a simmering stew, biting into a carrot, chewing and swallowing, feeling the sense of satisfaction as outer elements nourish and strengthen our inner being. Even the best menu is a pale and superficial imitation of enjoying a delicious bowl of soup. Just having a conceptual belief in basic goodness doesn't provide real spiritual nourishment.

The two most important aspects of the path of awakening, then, are nature and training. Both are essential. Without a natural interest in meditation, we cannot begin, continue, or reach the goal; without actually setting out on the journey to awakening, we will never arrive. Wakefulness is natural—this is the essential point, and we need to actually walk the path of meditation. Confidence in our original nature comes from skillfully combining these two.

2 Natural Training

I WANT TO EMPHASIZE that this approach to meditation and the spiritual path is supremely practical. The most practical basis for traveling the spiritual path is to begin with understanding. Where are we going, why are we going there, and how should we proceed? Taking time to contemplate and strengthen our understanding will serve us well; it's like gathering good food and water for the challenges of traveling, provisions for the journey ahead. We may feel impatient to get on with it already; after all, isn't the real point just to do it? The problem with "just do it" approaches to practice is that, by journeying without a map or sense of direction, we usually end up confused somewhere along the way: just do what? The goal of this journey is swiftly reached through joining "strong confidence in our original nature" (in the words of Shunryu Suzuki) with training in meditation.

Human beings are natural meditators. Traditionally it has been said that just as birds naturally fly and fish naturally swim, human beings are naturally awake. Presence is part of our human birthright. Meditating is the direct expression of our inherent wakefulness.

Trungpa Rinpoche's first book in English was called *Meditation in Action*. For years this title puzzled and intrigued me. I read and reread this book, wondering: How could you have meditation while doing things? Didn't meditation mean sitting still and stopping thoughts? How could you have that while making breakfast or during a difficult budget meeting? My own initial puzzlement reflects a common misunderstanding of meditation and the spiritual path overall: many of us approach meditation practice as a separate activity, segregated from our ordinary lives. In part this may reflect our learning the practice in isolated retreat settings—away from the ordinary situations of daily life. We go to a meditation or yoga center in the country, for a weekend or longer, in quiet natural surroundings away from the noise of traffic and the speed of the city. We may have extended periods of silence, abstaining from e-mail and telephone contact, and we practice for hours every day. This is helpful in providing an environment of strong support for being present, for establishing the good ground of a daily meditation practice. As a result, we notice our own experience with greater depth and subtlety, somewhat awake at last!

The downside of retreats is the subtle implication that meditation and spirituality are special activities—set apart from deadlines and dirty dishes, removed from freeways and year-end fiscal reports. We may approach meditation practice as an extraordinary activity, rare and elevated—as though the path were about becoming the spiritual equivalent of an Olympic gymnast. Such an approach belies the utter naturalness of meditation. Viewing spiritual practice in this way, we short-circuit the possibilities for "meditation in action." If meditation is truly the expression of our original nature, then that nature can be expressed wherever we are, at any moment. At home with family, at work, in a movie theater, or listening to music—wakefulness is there, and this wakefulness is the way.

The way of natural wakefulness finds spiritual nourishment in being with others, in experiences of living and working in community: our neighborhoods, online chat groups and wikis, the people we work with and relax with in play and sports. Our original nature is a fundamental human-heartedness, the empathy of our basic humanity. There is something in us that deeply appreciates and enjoys friendship, companions, family connections. Therefore, natural wakefulness flowers as the experience of being in community.

For us as practitioners—that is, as people interested in the experience-based practice of meditation—this fundamental teaching of joining original nature and mind-training is of much more than mere theoretical interest. The practical importance of this approach, this view of meditation, is that because we are going *with* the grain of our being we can afford to be gentle in all the aspects of our training. Particularly, our approach to training ourselves through meditation can be infused throughout with gentleness. This way of awakening is gentle in the beginning, gentle in the middle, and gentle in the end. Gentleness expresses confidence in the inherent goodness of our original nature. We don't need to aggressively grasp after higher states of consciousness—the light touch of awareness is all that is needed. We don't need to force the rays of the sun to radiate—radiating warmth and light is the spontaneous practice of the sun.

On the other hand, if we approach meditation as an extraordinarily difficult, special mental accomplishment—a rare state of being that only one or two people in all of history have ever achieved—we set ourselves up for frustration. We are focusing on what we are not yet, instead of appreciating what we are. Approaching meditation as an unusual state to achieve through extraordinary mental gymnastics is like setting out one fine day to teach a pig to fly. We've heard that flying is great; we've seen the birds swooping and soaring—what a noble, awesome achievement! Of course, it will take immense effort and force, possibly even a slight bit of aggression. (After all, don't they say, "No pain, no gain"?) In our frustration, we may even end up yelling at the pig: "Get up, up, up!" In the end we will inevitably suffer disappointment, in spite of all our hard work. Probably we will only succeed in annoying the pig. This is because we are engaged in a futile attempt to go against the naturally occurring order of things. (This natural order of things is one meaning of the Sanskrit word *dharma*.) However hard we try, we cannot turn ourselves into what we are not. When we try to do so, all of nature seems arranged against us. We end up fighting a losing battle with our own nature.

Thank (basic) goodness, walking the spiritual path is not a matter of achieving the impossible. If, instead, we approach meditation as a process of going with our natural tendencies, gentleness is more than enough. A light touch is sufficient. Ease and a sense of well-being in meditation practice are signs of this supremely skillful approach to working with ourselves. It's like watching an elegant dancer move across the floor combining the natural force of gravity with grace. Walking is artfully controlled falling. Similarly, meditation is an art of doing what comes naturally, while training ourselves in our own goodness—following gravity and riding the waves at once.

ALWAYS JUST A STEP AWAY

I grew up hearing many stories of my father's athletic prowess as a star basketball player. He had a quick first step, and he could magically leap for the goal. When I turned to contemplating meditation practice in my twenties, it was confusing at first to shift my attitude from trying to achieve a peak experience to appreciating the valley of nothing special. My meditation teacher's helpful emphasis that meditation is not a matter of mental gymnastics was crucial for me in making that shift, in transforming my view. Many people, however, do approach meditation or walking the spiritual path as though it were something like accomplishing the Olympic level of mental gymnastics—very few ordinary beings need apply. This narrow view suggests that we all need to become spiritual superstars—while cynically mocking the very slim possibility of this actually occurring. If, instead, we regard ourselves as always, at most, just one step away from the natural noticing that is the essence of meditating, it's as though we have already begun on the path even before we formally sit down to meditate. After all, when did we first begin noticing our minds and bodies, our emotions and the world around us? When did we first hear a songbird or see the stars? That's when we began the path of meditation.

Moments of such natural meditation are happening to us all the time. We pause at a stop sign while driving or taking a walk, and just for a moment, preoccupations of that important meeting tomorrow or memories of yesterday's flood of e-mails fall away. We are simply there, noticing other walkers and drivers, cars and sunlight, clouds and trees. A dog barks, and in the distance we can hear a siren. For a fleeting moment we have a more intense experience of simple presence. Then, for most of us, mentally it's back to the races—the future, the past, yesterday, last week, I forgot to call my mother, tomorrow, this afternoon, I'll be late, then the quarterly report will be late, whose fault is it really? And so on.

NOT TOO TIGHT, NOT TOO LOOSE

There is a story that a musician—a sitar player—came to the Buddha seeking meditation instruction: "How should I hold my mind in meditation?" The Buddha answered by drawing an example from the musician's own life (that is, the natural meditation practice that he was already engaged in): "How would you tune the strings of your sitar? Would you wind them until they are too tight, so that the notes will be sharp? Or would you unwind them until they are way too loose, and all the notes are flat?" Of course, the musician replied: "I would tune it so that the strings are not too tight and not too loose." "Just so," said the Awakened One, "tune your mind in meditation by holding it not too tightly and not too loosely."

This simple yet profound meditation instruction is another expression of the middle path of practice. Each time we sit down to meditate we are rediscovering the meaning of "not too tight, not too loose" for ourselves in our sitting practice. Yesterday's sense of precision and crisp attention to the details of our experience—a sound, an itch, a feeling, a smell, a thought—may be out of reach today. As we sometimes say, "It's just not happening."

We may need to soften and loosen and widen our attention, not trying quite so hard to make today's experience the same as yesterday's good meditation session. The unskillful approach to meditating is to try to make the present like the past, trying to reproduce pleasing moments from previous meditation sessions. The reason this meditation-as-manipulation scenario sounds so familiar is because this strong mental habit of trying to "fix" things carries over from the rest of our life. In contrast, the skillful approach to meditation is to appreciate what is naturally unfolding.

On the other hand, if we are simply sitting and singing ourselves a mental lullaby, while allowing the web of overlapping daydream after daydream to wrap ever more firmly around us like an old, fuzzy blanket, we should sound a wake-up call and apply more effort in the practice. Yesterday's just-right session may be today's too-lax meditation; suddenly we realize that we're coasting. Sometimes we need tightening up rather than letting go and loosening.

KNOWING WHAT IS HAPPENING

What is it that notices that we are trying too hard to force our mind to stay (and not trusting the mind's original wakefulness and natural stability)? What is it that knows that we are lazily letting our mind drift into dullness and mental fogginess (and not trusting the need to apply ourselves)? What is it that sees all our states of mind vividly—both our distractions and our clarity? We call this faculty of mind "natural wakefulness"—it knows what is happening in our meditation and allows us to adjust accordingly. Like Santa in the lyrics of the Christmas song: it knows when we've been drowsy; it knows when we've been awake.

It also knows what's going on in ordinary life situations, such as when we are veering to the left or the right while driving on the freeway, or if a note on a guitar is too sharp or flat. This inborn knowing is a very useful capacity. Without it, we cannot guide ourselves on the path. With it—and remember, we have it already—we can always find our way. Suzuki Roshi reminded us of the utter naturalness of the path when he said: "If you can taste the water you're drinking, you are all right."

Meditation involves training the mind by placing the natural attention. We train by being mindful of the body, for example, while sitting, walking, or standing. We place the awareness on an object of focus, and then let the attention stay there. As in the title of one of Pema Chödrön's weekends, we are "learning to stay." When we hold the mind too tightly to the object of meditation, we are forgetting the naturalness of being awake, the mind's innate ability to stay. Paying attention and being present are intimately familiar experiences, already close to us, not foreign or exotic states of mind. These qualities of mind are more like a family house pet, our favorite cat or dog, much more like these familiar companions than a giraffe or a leopard. Any lack of gentleness—aggressively forcing ourselves to be present—expresses lack of confidence in the mind's original nature.

On the other hand, sitting in a lackadaisical style suggests the need to engage the wisdom of training, taming the wildness of mind through the discipline of applying the instructions. What is the primary instruction? Notice what is happening right now, including the habitual drift into thoughts of the past or future, and then, if you are distracted from this noticing, return the attention to the present. The present is an ever-changing kaleidoscope of activity; the past is a pale copy of a memory of a dream.

Again we see that achieving the full beauty of this dance requires two partners; it's a duet, not a solo. We can confidently walk the spiritual path of awakening using our two legs of original nature and training through meditation.

A WIDER SENSE OF TRAINING

"Training" has many meanings—and our experience with training has a much longer history in our lives than we might realize. We can get physical training at a gym or yoga studio, professional training in a school, and training of the mind at a meditation center. But in a wider sense, we have also been training our body and mind just by living our life. When we were first taught to say "good morning" and "good night," when we went to a childhood friend's birthday party and someone suggested we take along a gift, when we went to our grandmother's funeral and first experienced human grief—all these experiences were shaping our heart, our mind, our life. Since we were not born speaking a particular language or knowing the customs of our culture, these things are acquired knowledge, abilities we gain through learning and training. I still have vivid memories from my childhood of my mother's and aunts' wails of grief after my uncle was killed suddenly in a head-on automobile collision. It left a strong impression: this is how we mourn our dead.

In this wider sense, our entire life has been training. The question is: training in what? This question means: training in which direction? If we train ourselves to reach for a snack or pick up the phone to text-message whenever we feel frightened or bored, this is definitely training. The next time we feel uncomfortable we will also tend to reach for some comfort outside ourselves, eventually establishing a deeply ingrained habit, another brick in the wall of our mental prison. Are we training in how to distract ourselves from inner discomfort or anxiety? Are we training in numbing ourselves in the face of fear, or training in waking up? Training in opening the heart, or training in shutting down?

When we first sit down to meditate—and later when we return to the cushion—we can immediately recognize that we are not starting with a clean slate. If we've fallen in love, then the glow of passion and romance will deliciously perfume our meditation experience. If we've had a particularly stressful week at work, then our Saturday morning meditation session may have some of the irritating flavor of recent conflicts and disagreements. We may find ourselves replaying difficult conversations repeatedly—in a tape loop of irritation. A friend who worked as an accountant once told me that his discursive thoughts in meditation during tax season were often exclamations in numbers: "534! 63,000! 10, 10, 10!" Whatever the previous day, week, month, year, decade have brought—it is immediately clear that our minds are already in motion, already have movement and momentum in a particular direction before we sit down. Our experience when we sit down to meditate—whether we've been sitting for thirty minutes or thirty years—will often reflect our previous physical and mental "training."

In other words, the wildness of mind that we experience when we sit quietly noticing our body and breathing for five minutes is the result of everything we've been doing before those five minutes. Frequently we discover that our minds do not rest in radiant contentment for the entire meditation session. Why not? Because we have been training for years in desiring, reaching, grasping, getting, and then wanting more, and then, of course, more—all reinforcing the underlying feeling that this moment is not enough. This pervasive feeling of something lacking, something missing ("not enough, not enough, when can I get something else, something different, something better?") is itself a powerfully motivating force. This is what we notice when we simply sit quietly with ourselves for even a few moments: we experience the accumulated momentum of mental noise, booming and buzzing. We notice how strongly we are trained to want something different from what is happening. We notice that our minds are very well trained in dissatisfaction and distraction. Almost always our focus is on something else—not this. We seek another moment of greater happiness—not this moment. Contentment seems always elsewhere—never here.

AWARENESS
We're Not So Distracted after All, Are We?

Remember that an important step in waking up is discovering, again and again, the ongoing rush and flow of mental activity. These thoughts and emotions and inner soap operas are usually a large part of our waking dream, our sleepwalking state. We cannot wake up without seeing our spiritual sleep clearly. Seeing mind's wildness close-up and in person is actually a sign of progress on the path.

If we notice distraction, we are not so distracted after all, are we? Consider the encouraging teaching: "That which sees confusion is not itself confused." We could celebrate the clarity that sees confusion clearly. There can be discouragement that the path seems such a lengthy journey, with pitfalls and roadblocks and so many obstacles. Who would have thought it would be so challenging? Were there really these many obstacles to waking up before we began practicing meditation?

When we shine a bright flashlight into a crowded, dark basement, we might suddenly see all the old furniture stored there. The light doesn't produce the furniture—but it does allow us not to trip over that wooden rocker in the corner, not to bump into the dusty couch. Seeing the obstacles clearly allows us to move, gracefully and with ease, through the crowded space of the room.

Discouragement comes from overemphasizing the strong grip of our habitual patterns, rather than rejoicing in the awakened potential that sees these patterns directly. One day, in the middle of an argument about money with a close friend, we step back for just a moment to notice the neurotic states of mind brought up by conflict. We see—we can almost taste it— the strong tendency to find fault, to blame, to harshly judge others and ourselves. We observe ourselves climbing on the roller-coaster ride of pride ("I'm right") to insecurity ("I might be wrong; I've been wrong before") to arrogance ("But I must be right; after all, I'm me!"). We already know what comes next on that ride. Gradually, and then with increasing frequency, we see that we are noticing ourselves and our familiar world in a new way, from a slightly different vantage point—like strong beams of sunlight illuminating dust motes in a room. This spacious, clear seeing of the patterns of confusion is itself liberation, the natural path of awakening.

3 Mindful Open Presence
A Gentle Way of Training

I SOMETIMES WORRY THAT THE EMPHASIS we often place on "knowing" in paths to spiritual awakening loses sight of our equally important capacity for caring. As one of my students in a college seminar said to me recently, "We don't really care what you know, until we know what you care about." Well said. This chapter is about mindfulness meditation—as a gentle way of training and encouraging our natural sense of presence. "Presence" means both an embodied sense of being and an emotionally available responsiveness. The ability to respond effectively to the suffering in our world is based on mindfulness. Our approach is cultivating mindful caring as the basis for kindness in living and working with others.

Mindfulness means attention. Mindfulness means that the mind is fully present, awake within a given activity. It means that when you are washing your face in the morning, you actually feel the slippery soap and the warm water splashing in your hands. Don't we feel all those sensations anyway? All too often, however, direct experience of the real-time present is replaced, forgotten, hastily bypassed. In our rush to get to the next moment, we substitute a fantasy life, an imagined double in the future, for the actual life we are living. I've washed my face thousands of times, and I'm bored with it, so instead I'm already caught up in planning and rehearsing what I need to say later this morning at the 9:30 meeting. Which is more real—my presence at the sink or my ideas about this morning's agenda? Mindfulness lets us reclaim the lives we are actually living.

You might wonder why it's more important to attend to the splash of warm water than to prepare for a meeting. The essential connection here is to see that being present while washing my face leads to more presence in the morning meeting. If we'd like greater engagement with the more important moments of life, we could start by engaging, leaning into, the ordinary, taken-for-granted, nothing special moments along the way. The reverse is also true: further ingraining the habit of being elsewhere will likely carry over into our meeting, where we may find ourselves worrying about the conference call we have later that afternoon. Then, during the conference call, we're already anxiously making mental notes about getting dinner for the kids. Absentmindedness—what Harvard psychologist Ellen Langer calls "mindlessness"—is a mental habit, deeply ingrained. Training in mindfulness reverses this pattern. Presence arises through training in awareness of the moment.

Mindfulness applies at home no less than in the workplace. When a family member—for instance, our teenage daughter or son—wants to talk with us, we need to be fully present in mind and heart to actually hear what they're saying—and what they're not saying. If our attention is elsewhere, "elsewhen" ("what's going to happen after she graduates next year?"), there are many fewer chances for a meaningful conversation—for the bright spark of genuine communication. It's as though one of the parties is talking while the other is flickering in and out of the room as in an old science-fiction movie, a ghostly presence at best. "Dad, you're not really listening to me!" "Mom, can't you hear what I'm saying?" Any deeper listening—and so too the possibility of mutual transformation, of communication that changes us—is grounded in mindful, open presence. This deeper communication is the basis of sane communities.

When we think about the value of simple presence for our daily lives—remembering how much we care about our loved ones and want them to be happy—we are moved to engage a discipline. We may approach having a sitting practice as something like physical exercise or daily dental flossing, a useful part of our regular mental hygiene. Yet mindfulness is also natural to us; we already have some innate awareness. After all, without attention how would we notice the switch to turn the lights on? How would we have picked up this book? Attention—the ability to be aware in the present—is one of our most precious faculties, inborn, yet mostly undeveloped. Mindfulness is an inner natural resource; it has vast yet largely untapped potential for real benefit in our lives and the lives of those around us. Meditation training simply develops this inherent human potential for compassionate wakefulness.

Our training in mindfulness begins with and returns to understanding. It's vitally important to clarify what mindfulness is—and what it is not. Otherwise, how will we know what we're doing, whether we're getting closer or farther away from genuine awakening? Here again just doing it is not enough. It would be as though someone walked into our morning meeting and urged us all to "Go, go, let's go!" We would feel the need to know, at the very least, something about where we're going. It would also help to have a sense of why we're going: Is there an important meeting elsewhere? Is there a fire in the building? We rouse our motivation for engaging in meditation training by thinking over the benefits to ourselves and others of mindful presence—as well as the high costs of mindlessness. This is contemplation—thinking it over before we begin the actual mindfulness training. Meditation may be the legs of that training, but contemplative study provides the eyes.

■ EXERCISE: BARE ATTENTION

Training in mindfulness uses our "bare attention." Here "bare" means simple, direct, uncovered. We say, "I touched it with my bare hand—no gloves on." Bare attention is achieved by using our natural consciousness—without additives. It's important to distinguish this direct attention, the essence of right mindfulness, from thinking about a sensation or perception. Here is an exercise to clarify this crucial point, to increase our understanding of the practice.

Take an orange, peel it, and place it before you in slices or sections. Now slowly pick up a piece of the fruit, smell it, and place it in your mouth to begin chewing—slowly. Notice the juices and the texture of the fruit in your mouth, the taste, and after you swallow, any lingering aftertaste. Try it again—one more piece of fruit, first the fragrance, if any, the texture in the mouth, the liquid released on chewing, the taste, and aftertaste. This is an exercise in paying bare attention to eating a piece of fruit.

Now—in order to highlight the difference between mindfulness of eating and *thinking* about eating: sit still for a moment and just remember the taste of the fruit. Bring it to mind as vividly as possible, what it felt like, what it tasted like. As well, expand your feelings and thoughts about the (remembered) taste of the fruit: "I really liked that orange; I should get more of them—where was it I bought them, how much were they? I'd like more of them, maybe a half dozen or so, soon." Or, mentally talk to yourself about the disappointment of oranges these days: "That wasn't a very good orange, was it? Not much flavor at all. I'm sorry I bought those—a stupid mistake, and I must remember not to visit the fruit section of that new store again. I'm tired of oranges anyway—maybe kiwis?"

Notice that these are thoughts—and thoughts about a memory. These thoughts may be based on a pleasurable memory—"I liked that orange"—or a disappointing memory—"I didn't like that piece of fruit"—but in either case they are equally thoughts.

Now pick up another piece of fruit and taste it again, actually, in real time, not a remembered moment from the past. Be as present as you can with the simple, unadorned sensations of smelling, biting, tasting, chewing, swallowing. Notice how different this bare attention to eating a piece of fruit is from all our thoughts about oranges. Sensing this obvious difference is the basis for mindfulness meditation practice. We place our bare attention on a simple sensation—like taste—and then let mindfulness rest there, stay there, as long as it lasts. This is the heart of the practice of meditation.

SO WHAT?

Often there are lingering doubts about the practical value of what we're cultivating in this exercise. At meditation retreats, someone will often say something like: "So, I'm understanding mindfulness as a kind of naked attention to the present, but why, aside from the benefit of tasting my food more, would I want to cultivate this?" In a sense, our understanding of the path is made of questions like this. We mix our experience of daily life and practice with inquiry.

Think back to that morning meeting in which we were so

lost in thought about the afternoon conference call that we missed the most important moment of the morning's presentation. Think back to quiet conversations we've had in which our overlapping thoughts and reactions to what a friend or family member is saying block our direct awareness of what they are actually saying. As with the orange, we take our thoughts about a remembered event as reality. We may be thinking about what we're going to say next and miss the obvious fact that it no longer needs saying! Often our loved ones are asking us for a deeper, mindful listening.

Mindfulness opens the doorway into a fuller experience of the heart, the richly rewarding yet volatile realm of emotions. The practice of being present is valuable not only for the mental sharpness it brings to decision-making but also for providing fertile ground for the development of "emotional intelligence." This is psychologist Daniel Goleman's phrase for what many traditions speak of as "the wisdom of the heart." Being present is absolutely necessary to sense the situation, feel what is needed, and let our care and concern find the most skillful way to help.

The group meditation retreats I lead usually include one-to-one conversations with each of the participants about the experiential journey they are making. I have learned to do this from my own teachers, who counseled that generally, meditation instruction cannot be given in a class. There has to be a personal relationship between teacher and student. These practice conversations help to focus the general, traditional meditation instructions in a more precise and personally meaningful way.

In the first years of guiding and encouraging people along their meditative journeys, I often found myself stumbling over my own eagerness to be helpful. Mary would come in to talk with me about her morning sessions of mindfulness meditation. We sit, bow to each other in the traditional gesture of mutual respect—and wait a moment in silence. As usual, there have been some ups and downs, but, overall, she feels that the practice is going well, nodding her head affirmatively as she says this. Another pause. "Though," she adds in a softer voice, "it's still unsatisfying somehow. Sometimes there's a feeling of skating along on the surface of my experience, not breaking the ice to get down to any real depth of feeling." I nod, acknowledging the problem—and then wait to see what comes next. In the space between us, there is room for whatever needs to emerge to do so—and, after a few moments Mary begins crying softly, saying that she misses her husband, who recently passed away from lung cancer. Her grief is almost palpable and seems to fill the room. The strongest temptation I feel at this moment is to search quickly through my memory for the appropriate teaching from the vast wisdom tradition of compassion. What do the teachings have to say, I wonder, that will alleviate Mary's suffering and allow her to get on with her life? There are teachings on impermanence—on the unchanging fact that everything changes. There are teachings on non-attachment and letting go, as well as suggestions of ways to accept and work with uncomfortable emotions. Other teachings stress the importance of using painful situations to realize greater compassion through empathizing with the suffering of the many, many others who also grieve the loss of a loved one.

As we sit quietly with each other, I consider these and other teachings for several moments, unsure what to say to be helpful. Slowly it dawns that this very eagerness to do something, to apply an antidote or a remedy, overshoots the mark of simple presence and emotional openness. Finally I say to myself, "None of this strategizing works; what she wants is just someone to be present, to share her experience of sadness." I realize that I'm mistakenly setting out on a fix-it project—as though there is something wrong with the grief Mary is feeling. This haste to "cure" her emotional distress is well-meaning but fundamentally aggressive in its drive to change her experience from what it is.

The awakened heart of mindfulness, on the other hand, allows me simply to be with Mary's feeling of sadness—as well as to make friends with my own uncomfortable feelings in the presence of such depth of feeling. It's an awkward and tender moment in which two people feel the vulnerability of the human heart. Of course we all wish that our loved ones would not die—as absurd as that wish surely is for mortal beings. Mindfulness gives a dignity to the experience of sharp and painful grief—it's enough in itself; it does not need changing or correcting or a spiritual cure. I appreciate the title of one of Sakyong Mipham's seminars on meditation; he called it "Being Human." Mindfulness is appreciating the fullness of being human.

HARMONY OF BODY AND MIND

Remember our imagined encounter with an awakened being walking gracefully up and down the aisles of the local market? There was something in the way they moved. We were struck by the embodied presence there. Someone moving with synchronized awareness and body is graceful, stable yet unburdened, simultaneously grounded and light. We sometimes see this quality in great athletes—but it can be part of an ordinary embodied presence as well.

Certainly, the absence of this quality is striking. When our mind is elsewhere and "elsewhen," while our body trundles along in the present, our motions are jerky. We carry our body around like a sack of potatoes we're stuck with lugging from one place to another. Mindfulness of body, of heart, and of mind are taught in a sequence but the aim is to be fully present physically, emotionally, and mentally all together at once.

This integrated state of being—embodied presence—is both stable and steady as well as open and vulnerable. When I was speaking with Mary and empathizing with her grief, both qualities were present. She needed the mirroring back to her of a sense of stability, so that her own steadiness of heart and mind could be more available to experience. At the same time, she needed an open, sympathetic listener—able to feel and share in her experience of grief. Both strength and emotional availability are cultivated in meditation practice. Let's look now at more specifics of how mindfulness-awareness practice actually works.

4 Home Ground

Resting Attention in the Body

TO TRAIN IN THE PRACTICE OF MINDFULNESS, we take our natural ability to pay attention, place the mind on a particular object, and let it stay there. This is called resting the mind. It's essentially the same as when we practiced awareness of eating a piece of fruit: we brought our attention to the sensations of chewing and tasting the orange and stayed with those. Now we are moving to a firm basis for our meditation, one that lasts longer and is more stable than the quickly passing taste of a piece of fruit. The traditional instructions handed down in the long lineage of meditators—from the Buddha to present-day teachers—recommend using what we already are, what we already have available to us now, as the best basis for practice.

What do we have to work with? We are bodies, feelings, minds, and sense perceptions—and so these are available to us to use as foundations for building the house of meditation. The body comes first as the most tangible aspect of our existence—almost everywhere we go, the body is with us. As the saying goes: "Wherever you go, there you are." We use this very familiar aspect of human life—the physical aspect of being human—as the basis of our meditation practice.

Although we are beginning with the body, eventually we will include our emotions and thoughts, mental activity, and sense perceptions as further fuel for the fire of mindfulness. But the body provides the fundamental home ground. Mindfulness of body forms the basis for the entire meditative journey.

Because this foundation of all our practice is so important, we will focus on this topic for three sessions. The meditation instructions and exercises could be engaged in one session per day over the next three days (or, if you prefer, all in a single, longer period on the same day). Each session includes: (1) instruction and reminders of the overall approach (looking forward), (2) a guided exercise in actually doing it (the practice itself), and then (3) some reflection on the process we've just engaged in (looking back). Either morning or evening for these sessions is fine, but allow yourself fifteen to twenty minutes for each: enough time to read through the instructions, practice the exercise, and think back over what you've just experienced. Now let's begin.

SESSION 1 *Mindfulness of Body*

The instructions for practicing mindfulness of body are simple: we place our attention in the physical form. We can do this meditation while sitting, standing, walking, or lying down. It's the same as the bare attention to eating a piece of fruit: being mindful of the body involves resting our naked, direct awareness on the actual body, this body, the physical form that we have and are. Our first session, awakening mindfulness of body, will consist of a threefold series of exercises that each time take us deeper into the practice.

LOOKING FORWARD

As with the fruit exercise, we could contrast this more direct experience of our body—achieved through bare attention or mindfulness of our physical experience—with thinking about the body. We all have a buzzing swarm of ideas and concepts that surround our bodies: we love our bodies; surely, they are dear to us. (After all, as the old joke goes, without our bodies, we'd be dead.) We also have judgments and fears about our bodies. Sometimes bodies are unruly, unpredictable, and unreliable when it comes to doing just what we'd like them to do at the moment. If we have inherited ideas from certain religious traditions, we may regard our bodies with lingering feelings of shame or embarrassment. On the other hand, we may hold the view that the body is sacred, the carrier of embodied wisdom, a sensual path to enlightenment itself. As well, our bodies are almost always associated, implicitly if not overtly, with sexuality—a rich arena for feelings, ideas, and strong judgments; for both anxious control and spontaneous attractions. What is the right body to have? In other words, what is our body ideal? What kind of body do we desire?

Aside from the ideas inherited from various religious traditions, the most secular among us will tend to fall into physical comparison and criticism: Is my body as attractive, as beautiful, as strong and fit as it once was? Is my body as good as others' bodies? Is my body really healthy? As healthy as it should be, as healthy as hers, as his? Too much, too little, excessive, inadequate, plus-size and petite—all these concepts and evaluations of our bodies come along with us as we enter a yoga class or go jogging, change diets or weigh ourselves in the morning. We all inherit a powerful set of cultural concepts of the body; these shape our psychological experience of being embodied.

Take a moment to self-reflect: how do you feel about your body, right now? Trungpa Rinpoche spoke of a "psychosomatic body." This is the body surrounded by a big net of mental attitudes about bodies that we bring to the practice of mindfulness of body.

This contemplation begins with acknowledging our thoughts and concepts about the body, and then, as much as possible, feeling the body itself. There is no need to do battle with the various ideas and judgments; we notice these thoughts and concepts and then simply step through them, like stepping through a small swarm of gnats, to move closer to resting the mind in our actual physical being. The next step is to stand and deliver: it's time to actually do it.

■ EXERCISE: AWAKENING MINDFULNESS OF BODY

For this exercise, it's better if you're comfortably dressed—you might want to loosen your belt a little and remove your jacket or any tight-fitting articles of clothing. Shoes on or off, as you like—but you need a chair with a firm seat (not an easy chair or a couch) for the sitting portion of the exercise. Place the chair nearby, but begin the exercise by standing.

1. Stand with your feet comfortably apart, with hands resting at your sides; let them fall naturally. Check your knees to see that they are not rigidly locked; find a middle position—neither bent nor locked. Your shoulders should be back, your head level, with the chin slightly down. Eyes should be open but downcast. The primary instruction is to stand here and feel the body.

What does that really mean? How do we bring attention to the feeling of the body? It may help to first scan the parts of the body, beginning with the feet, the ankles, the calves, the knees, the thighs, the pelvic area, the waist, and so on. Slowly move the focus of your attention up the back of the body (an area that is often neglected, left outside the warmth of our attention). Move the focus of your attention up the back and then slowly down the front, taking your time, not hurrying but not lingering too long either. When you've completed one whole cycle—scanning with the attention up the back and down the front, then simply stand with your attention in the body. Feel any specific sensations that arise—such as your feet on the floor, and the weight of the body standing. As much as you can, feel the whole body at once, a global sense of the body. Do this for two or three minutes, now.

2. Next, we'll do a similar mindfulness-of-body exercise while seated. Sit comfortably in your chair, your back away from the back of the chair (so that you are self-supporting), your feet flat on the floor. Place your hands, palms down, on your thighs, and again lower your chin slightly (there is more tendency to daydream when the chin is tilted up). If your eyes remain open, let your gaze fall toward the floor—to encourage the mind to be present in the body. Now, once again, the primary instruction is to sit here and feel your body. Before we were practicing mindfulness of the standing body; now we are practicing mindfulness of the sitting body.

As with the mindfulness-of-body standing meditation, it may help to attune to the sitting practice of meditation by way of a body scan. First, feel the bottoms of your feet on the floor. Feel the parts of your legs—the ankles, calves, thighs. Feel the waist—and relax any excess tension there as well. Feel the torso, the lower back, the upper back, and the shoulders, relaxing these areas as much as you can as you attend to them. Feel the back of the neck, the back of the head, the top of the head, the forehead. Relax the eyes, cheeks, and jaws. Pay particular attention to unclenching the jaws. Relax. The mouth could be slightly open. Feel the front of the body, the stomach, the waist, and the flat bottom pressing on the chair. Having felt the parts of the body—articulating the attention to the sitting body—then bring your attention to the whole body at once, the global body. Again, sit in mindfulness meditation for five minutes.

During this time, if you find your attention wandering elsewhere—to this coming weekend's big birthday gathering, for example—gently return attention to the seated body. Do this again and again, as needed. The mind has been trained to wander—like an endless channel surfer, never resting from its fruitless quest for lasting satisfaction from something outside. Now we are training it (re-training it, really) to stay in, to rest and find contentment within, our present experience. Stay with the bare sensation of the body as long as you can. That's it.

3. Then, to conclude the exercise portion of this first session, return briefly to standing. Stand comfortably as before, paying particular attention to the alignment of the body—leaning neither forward nor back, not rigid and not slumping. As with sitting, treat the standing body as your familiar home ground, and return to it again and again. Here the mind is like a homing pigeon: it may circle up and around and away in flight for long moments, but eventually it always swoops back down to land. Once it lands, let it stay here as long as you can, without forcing it (aggression) or immediately cooking up further entertaining thoughts (indulgence). Let the mind be with the body: that's the key instruction.

LOOKING BACK

What were we just doing? We were training our minds to stay with the body, strengthening our mindfulness of body. This is a kind of "counter-training," for the mind has already been thoroughly trained in distraction, trained to chase after movement, constantly seeking change and something new. We rarely notice how repetitive, stale, and habitual this seeking truly is. Every time we watch televised or recorded images on a screen, we are reinforcing the hopping, skipping, and jumping quality of our attention, as it rapidly moves from one ad to another. First this and then that but now a new this! Because of this repetition, the mind has become accustomed to moving from object to object very quickly—superficially skimming the surface of our experience, always looking for something else, something more, something better. Distraction is married to dissatisfaction.

In contrast, by training the mind to stay, we are developing its natural stability, ripening its innate potential for steadiness. This opens into a deeper tasting of our experience—even ordinary rice and vegetables for lunch can be spiritually nourishing, deeply satisfying. Sometimes I am surprised to suddenly remember this simplicity during group retreats. The whole emphasis shifts. Instead of wondering how many stars for that new restaurant, I return to simply tasting this. Home ground.

Even before engaging the discipline of meditation, as we go to work in the morning our mindfulness rests for a moment on the clouds in the sky or a barking dog or a yellow traffic light, at least long enough to register what is happening. After all, without some natural mindfulness, how would we ever get to that birthday party or find our way home? In meditation, we take that innate yet flickering stability and allow it to grow—feeding it the nourishment of a daily mindfulness practice.

This quality of steadiness of mind can be very helpful to us—in personal relationships, in the workplace, at school, and at play. We notice that friends and family appreciate it if we stay present to hear what they're saying to us. (As opposed to that telltale question of mindlessness: "Sorry—what did you say?") Even our own bodies appreciate the sustained attention of mindfulness—as though we're listening in a deeper way to this fundamental dimension of our being for the first time. In this way, mind and body are being reintroduced to each other, as though after a long separation. Beyond the dualistic split, as Trungpa Rinpoche says, "In the dance of life, matter reflects mind, and mind reacts to matter. There is a continual exchange." This analogy of dynamic interaction beautifully describes the gradual unfolding of mindfulness practice: a process of increasing intimacy, where body and mind become close friends, harmonious companions, partners in a playful dance.

Sometimes we feel restless: when the instructions say to stand, we want to sit down, and when it says to sit, we feel like standing and stretching, running, or doing yoga. We may even begin to doubt our own potential: "Maybe I'm just not the kind of person who can do this meditation. Maybe I'm just not cut out to be a meditator?"

This mindfulness-awareness practice is an offering from the long lineage of compassionate meditation masters to people with busy, speedy, distracted minds. It's intended for women and men with wild minds like ourselves. After all, if our minds are already resting continually in a state of calm abiding, what would be the need for further training in stability? Training in resting the mind in the body is a highly recommended practice for the restless.

Meditation develops our basic appreciation for "what is." Our focus is usually divided—between awareness of what is happening and what we think should be occurring. "By now, I should be feeling my 'global body'—but I'm not. Thoughts are happening—and they shouldn't be. When does the exciting, ecstatic part of meditating kick in?" In each case, rely first on inquisitive attention to whatever is arising in body and mind. If you notice the front of the body but not the back, if you feel tired or anxious in a given session, if mind and body seem to be happily swimming along together, let it be that way. This letting be isn't the only method to apply in our practice—but it is the primary instruction.

SINKING DEEPER INTO MINDFULNESS OF BODY: LOOKING FORWARD

We embark on a second level of our mindfulness-of-body session by allowing ourselves to sink more deeply into the feelings and sensations of standing and sitting. Sakyong Mipham often describes meditation as a process of becoming familiar with our bodies and minds. This word, "familiar," has the same root as "family"—those we know most intimately, often from living in the same household. In the same way, we are deepening our awareness of our own bodies by living there, fully inhabiting our physical being, moving beyond mere superficial acquaintance toward intimate, direct knowledge.

We may discover that the body has an earthy aspect—it connects us with the earth and, like the earth, has a solid, elemental, and reliable quality. Trungpa Rinpoche describes tuning into the steadiness of the body as a "Sitting Bull" quality: "Sitting Bull is very solid and organic. You are definitely present, resting." In mindfulness-of-body practice, we use the body's natural weight and stability to steady the mind, to draw out the mind's own inherent groundedness. When body and mind truly meet, we feel like mountains meditating.

■ EXERCISE: SINKING DEEPER INTO MINDFULNESS OF BODY

1. This exercise begins with the sitting practice of meditation. Take a comfortable seat, feet flat on the floor as before, legs about shoulder-width apart. Again check that your back is self-supporting, not leaning on the back of the chair. This

gesture of self-reliance—independence—is key: you are taking responsibility for your own state of mind, and the posture
of the body expresses this personally proactive, take-charge
approach. Working with our minds is not up to anyone else.
In the practice of meditation, as Dzigar Kongtrül emphasizes, "It's up to you."

Having found a relaxed and restful position—with the
back not arched too much—again scan the body from toes
to head and back down to the feet again. Take your time—if
the mind strays, bring it back, and keep at it.

When you have completed this touching in with the various parts of the body, then let the mind rest in the feeling of
the whole body at once, the sense of the body as a unified
totality. Yes, there are many parts to the physical form, but
it's also one body. Place the mind in the body, and rest there
for several minutes.

There is a calmness in simply letting ourselves be, as we
are and where we are, not striving to be elsewhere or trying to
avoid anything. We're neither shying away from challenges
nor lunging after the next pleasure. Recognizing the basic
sanity of nonstruggle, of simply "letting be," we appreciate
the peacefulness of this moment. We could celebrate the
simplicity of pure being.

2. Now, please stand again, and take the standing meditation posture as before—steady (not rocking back and forth
or side to side), but also not rigid or tense (knees unlocked).
Again recall the main instruction: stand here and feel the body.
Include any momentary sensations that arise. Let whatever
thoughts arise simply come and go. As much as you can, stay
with the body.

Now within the sense of groundedness, resting in the
still, standing body, begin to notice the small movements of
the body, the process that we call breathing. Feel the expansion and contraction of your chest with each inhalation and

exhalation. Feel the air coming in through the nose and mouth and then going back out. Remember to be mindful of these sensations rather than merely mentally talking to yourself about them. Notice the mind's chatter, but lean in toward the actual physical sensations. Gently feel the body breathing air in, breathing air out, breathing in, breathing out. Breathing has a soothing rhythm, like the regular waves of an ocean. The breath, Suzuki Roshi said, is like a swinging door. Feel the back-and-forth swing of the breathing.

Stand and feel the back-and-forth movement of the body breathing for at least five minutes.

3. Conclude this exercise by again sitting down. Taking a moment to arrange a comfortable, upright, yet relaxed seat, let your attention fall into the seated body. When we are lost in thought, it is as though the mind is leaping, high-jumping, stretching up, up, and away from where we actually are. Take a moment now to reverse that habitual pattern—let the mind fall and settle down into the physical form. Appreciate the simple sense of being, and then, as with standing, include the movements of the chest and stomach, the series of small physical movements we call breathing, as part of the mindfulness-of-body meditation.

Traditionally, in the meditation instructions handed down from the Buddha, attention to breathing is understood as part of the overall practice of mindfulness of body. Sit here and feel the body breathing in (however short or long the breath, let it be that way) and breathing out (don't try to make the breath deeper or longer, just let it be however it is). Sometimes, depending on a host of other factors in our lives, like exercise and diet and the season, our breathing will be shallower; at other times breathing will be deeper, slower. For the purposes of cultivating mindfulness and awareness, it doesn't matter; this isn't yogic breathing or a deep-breathing exercise.

This is simply mindfulness of the body breathing: mindful of a short breath coming in, mindful of a short breath going out; mindful of a long breath coming in, mindful of a long breath going out. To conclude this exercise, sit for two or three minutes, being mindful of the seated body breathing.

SINKING DEEPER INTO MINDFULNESS OF BODY: LOOKING BACK

At this point we've added attention to our breathing to the basic practice of mindfulness of the body standing and sitting. It has been said that mindfulness of body connects us with the earth, and the breath is like wind moving over the earth. As air moves over the earth underneath the vast sky, we are harmoniously joining movement and stillness, presence and openness.

Sometimes mindfulness is approached as concentration, heavy-handedly trying to fix the attention on one object. In contrast, Trungpa Rinpoche placed particular emphasis on the expansive openness of meditation: "A quality of expansive awareness develops through mindfulness of body—a sense of being settled and of therefore being able to afford to open out." Here, settling down and opening out go hand in hand.

MINDFULNESS OF BODY, ON THE SPOT: LOOKING FORWARD

Before beginning the third and final level of our mindfulness-of-body practice, let's pause for a moment to think over what we're doing: what is the purpose of meditation? Why are we placing our attention in the body and letting it stay there? What are some of the benefits of a more embodied presence? Take a moment for self-reflection before you begin.

Make this contemplation as personal as you'd like—what are your motivations for engaging a meditation discipline? Why are you doing this? Without that felt personal sense of motivated interest and engagement, meditation remains something that someone else suggests that you do. Even if that someone else is the Buddha, unless we find what the Zen tradition calls our own "way-seeking heart-mind," the practice never really clicks. Motivation is the most important factor in the success or failure of meditation practice.

Having clicked, having dug down deep enough to feel the impulse to awaken in our own being, we can proceed with inner confidence. This digging-deeper process isn't a do-it-once-and-you're-done-forever engagement. Each time we sit down on our chair to meditate, we need to pause for a moment to reflect on our reasons for doing so. That puts some wind in our sails for the day's journey ahead.

In contemplating the purpose of meditation, it may help to recall the teachings and writings of great meditation masters. Trungpa Rinpoche spoke of the importance of synchronizing body and mind. This phrase is a wonderful description of the realization of mindfulness of body: "The ideal state of tranquility comes from experiencing body and mind being synchronized."

What does this mean? The word "synchronized" is from the Greek word for "time," *chronos,* the word at the root of several other English words such as chronicle, chronology, and chronic. Body and mind being synchronized means that they are both experienced in the same time, the same moment. What is that moment? When can body-mind synchronization occur? Now. Although the mind may seem to race ahead into next week, with plans for next month and next year, the body is really only present now. Their meeting can only take place when both are present—in nowness.

Our meditation practice has an on-the-spot flavor: we deal, as precisely as we can, with the challenges of body, breathing, and discursiveness right now. When mind races toward the future while the body is left behind in the present, we all become slightly more ghostlike presences, more and more mental bodies, much closer to being mere talking heads. In comparison, there is an almost tangible richness of experience, a fullness of heart and mind, when we actually stop for a moment to genuinely feel our body standing or sitting. Bringing body and mind together in the present moment is the essence of mindfulness of body.

■ EXERCISE: MINDFULNESS OF BODY, ON THE SPOT

1. Stand as before, feet comfortably apart, and gaze down. Take a moment to feel yourself in the standing meditation posture. Then go ahead and include mindfulness of the breathing in your overall awareness of the body standing. Stand this way, breathing naturally, and appreciating your mind settling into your body for five minutes.

2. Then sit down and arrange yourself comfortably on your seat. Again take a moment to feel your physical being, your embodied presence in the sitting posture—before rushing ahead to engage the breathing. Sit, and feel the body sitting. Remember: you are using this attunement to your physical being to ground yourself in the present, to arrive at a simple sense of being. Fully taking your seat in meditation means more than just parking your body in a particular posture, and then going elsewhere. Arrange the body in an upright yet relaxed position, and then feel the body in that posture.

3. Then include the mindfulness of the sitting body breathing, the full cycle of breathing in and out. Rest with this for

five to ten minutes, paying particular attention to the wandering movements of the attention.

Notice when your attention leaves the body for flights of fantasy and discursiveness: "I wonder what Connie is doing these days? She's probably still married to Paul. Is Henry really moving to L.A.? I can't believe he would really do it—it's so far away from his family. I wrote to Sandra and she hasn't returned my e-mail yet—why not?" Notice this subconscious mental gossip, recognize that the attention has swerved away from the physical presence of the body, and then gently return it to its landing pad—the body in sitting meditation posture. Do this again and again, however many times you recognize the mind's habit of distracting itself. When you return to the sensations of the body breathing, lean into those, training the mind to stay by elongating the moments of being present.

It can be helpful to accentuate the boundary between mindfulness of body and the jangling chatter of our inner conversation by making a mental note: saying "thinking," for instance, whenever you notice you've gotten lost and taken off on a long train ride of discursive thought. When you notice, just say to yourself, "thinking," and come back to the body breathing.

If you detect inner voices of discouragement and judgment and self-criticism ("What's wrong with me? Why am I not doing this right? Why won't my mind stay with the body?"), notice that chatter in the same way that you notice any other internal mental dialogue—with friendly interest and curiosity. Notice the mind's movement, say "thinking," and then return to the body breathing. Appreciate the moments of staying—the flowing, easeful quality of mind and body when they are in synch with each other—as well as the moments of jumping back and forth between past and present, future and present. As much as possible, enjoy the ups and downs of your meditative journey.

MINDFULNESS OF BODY, ON THE SPOT: LOOKING BACK

We cannot go back to yesterday's mindfulness session, or anticipate what will come up tomorrow, when we sit down today. Training our attention has a continually fresh and often surprising quality—it's a matter of being honest with ourselves about our actual experience in the moment. How is it now? And now? And now?

At the same time, it's also good to increase our sense of the long-term goals, the larger vision of meditation in action. We sit to make friends with ourselves, which can be the basis for more kindness, for the bravery and strength of patience, in what is an increasingly stressed-out world. Meditation is part of living a larger meditative life, our life in families and communities, among friends and relatives and the people we work with, in stores and companies, hospitals and schools. Being in the body attunes us to a fundamental, shared wisdom—something we have in common with all beings. Trungpa Rinpoche's book on making a sane society, *Shambhala: The Sacred Path of the Warrior,* is one of the best presentations of the connection between practicing meditation and bringing sanity to the larger communities we live in. It's a great guidebook for bringing awakened compassion to the world.

Let's conclude our series of exercises on mindfulness of body by contemplating this wider view of the practice of being human, of cultivating basic human-heartedness in order to share that humanity with others. From *Shambhala*: "Synchronizing mind and body . . . is a basic principle of how to be a human being . . . Synchronizing mind and body is also connected with how we synchronize or connect with the world, how we work with the world altogether." This simple gesture of embodied presence can be the basis of caring for the earth and all its living beings.

5 Dancing Stillness

*Helpful Hints on
Mindfulness of Body Meditation*

IN A FAMOUS MEDITATION TEACHING, the Awakened One guides his students into the practice of the four foundations of mindfulness: mindfulness of the body, mindfulness of feelings, mindfulness of the mind, and mindfulness of perceptions. Each of the four foundations serves as a basis, a platform, for mindfulness practice itself. We can base our cultivation of attention on these four factors. When we place our attention on the body, the emotions, and the mind, we are cultivating mindfulness within our own being.

The body, in particular, provides an ideal initial grounding principle for our practice, as we have just seen. Without the weight and stability of the body, our practice seems to float, uncertainly poised somewhere in midair—really neither here nor there. With our attention in the body, mindfulness itself seems to take on some much-needed weight, some substance and gravity. There is an old-fashioned way of expressing this, describing a woman or man as "a person of substance," meaning that they are not frivolously drifting along from one meaningless pursuit to another. Similarly, we might say that, through mindfulness of body, our meditation becomes "a practice of substance." Growing day by day, our flimsy mindfulness of body gradually takes on some needed weight and strength.

Overall, then, these foundations are handy places to establish our mindfulness. In contrast to what Trungpa Rinpoche called the "eternal hitchhiker" approach, we establish a campsite, pitch our tent, and perhaps eventually lay a foundation to build a home here. Each of the foundations is both something we already have—a mind, feelings, a body—and something we can use on the path of awakening. Through attending directly and consistently to our own being, we develop stability, a relation to liveliness and vital energies, and a connection with the spaciousness of mind itself.

At this point, you might be thinking something like, "even in those moments when I manage to place my attention on my body, it still seems like I have a lot of concepts. Sometimes I feel like I'm being mindful of my idea of my body. Is this a problem if it isn't really the *real* body I'm being mindful of?"

It's good that you recognize that, even in our practice of bare attention, there are still a lot of ideas about our body at work. It's insightful to see that, often, we're still talking to ourselves about our bodies instead of feeling the body directly. This is our ordinary condition—layers and layers and layers of conceptual overlays on the actual body. But perhaps—like the princess in the fairy tale who sleeps atop twenty mattresses and twenty featherbeds, but still feels the pea somewhere underneath her—occasionally we can have some sense of our actual body, underneath all these coverings.

Even though we are not constantly in full, direct, non-conceptual contact with our bodies, we're still leaning in that direction. As long as you understand that the direction of mindfulness practice is not toward more analysis or reflection or more theories and ideas about the body, as long as you aim toward bare attention, your practice of mindfulness of body is fine. Even though we are not yet in Buenos Aires, if you understand that, starting from Mexico City, we need to head south—not north—you are on the right road to meditation. As Tibet's greatest meditator, the yogi Milarepa, said, "Hasten slowly, and you will soon arrive."

Sometimes it's difficult to even find the breath or feel the breathing. You might feel too caught up in your mind—racing here and there like a roadrunner. Sometimes you might make the mistake of emphasizing the breath as in a deep-breathing exercise. When you recognize this overexertion, drop it—and breathe naturally.

Many of our questions about meditation circle around the issue of effort: how much effort to apply, what is too much effort. When are we trying so hard that we're getting in our own way? When are we not trying enough? There are many traditional teachings on right effort and even the mindfulness of effort itself, but the general pattern is that we need to apply more effort in the beginning and then gradually less as we proceed along the path. Sometimes this is even the pattern of a particular meditation session—we sit down, we actively and energetically engage the practice we're doing, we come back again and again—and then, at moments, we find ourselves simply sailing along—without needing to self-consciously monitor the process closely from moment to moment. We're not spacing out so much—and when discursive thoughts arise, we simply notice them and continue without much sense of interruption. Meditation becomes a natural, seamless process.

In a sense, we're moving from placing more emphasis on training—which is necessary at the beginning—to organically developing more trust in natural mindfulness. This corresponds to the overall arc of the spiritual journey we're making—from nature to training to nature. That is to say: our actual journey is from original nature, through "bad" training in aggressiveness and speed, through the restorative training in mindfulness, and so on, back to the original nature. It's like one of those heroic stories in which we leave our original home, journey through the woods, up and down over hill and dale, and eventually return home. In one sense we are certainly wiser for the journey we've made. In another sense, nothing—repeat, nothing—has been added. We've simply returned to the place of our beginning and known it fully for the first time.

The classic guidebook *Meditation in Action* describes the meditator's journey—from exertion in training to resting confidently in natural wakefulness: "At the beginning some effort is needed, but after practicing for a while the awareness is simply kept on the verge of the movement of breath; it just follows it quite naturally, and one is not trying particularly to bind the mind to breathing. One tries to feel the breath—outbreathing, inbreathing, outbreathing, inbreathing."

Just so: at the beginning, it would be sheer laziness not to apply the helpful antidote of effort, in remembering what we are trying to do—place the attention in the breathing body—and doing it. At other moments, there is no need to fiddle with our mindfulness, to try to improve it or "bind the mind to the breathing." It's swimming along with the stream, and there's no need to interfere by making extra effort. Instead one discovers a natural effort. There are moments when we come upon a spontaneous joy in meditating, like walking through dense woods that suddenly open onto a spacious meadow. To our surprise, given what sometimes seems like the wall-to-wall pervasiveness of speed and distraction, the mind actually enjoys being with the body.

WHY WON'T MY MIND STAY?

Question: I'm able to place my attention on my body breathing, but it just won't stay, at least not for very long. It doesn't seem to matter whether I'm standing or sitting, a few moments of mindfulness and being present, and then it's off to the races again. I find this frustrating; if the mind is by nature stable, clear, and strong—why won't it stay? As Sakyong Mipham says in *Turning the Mind into an Ally,* "The human mind is by nature joyous, calm, and very clear." OK, then, why does it wander so much? If it's so naturally calm and all, why doesn't it naturally stay with the body breathing?

Answer: Nature in the practical context of our training is the real testing ground of the truth of the teachings. Sakyong Mipham comments: "From a Buddhist point of view, human beings aren't intrinsically aggressive; we are inherently peaceful. This is sometimes hard to believe." There's a similarly incredible quality to the teaching that our mind has an inherent stability, especially when we place it on a firm foundation and see that it does everything except stay. It moves, it jumps, it runs here and there. Sometimes we wonder if the meditation teachings are describing the inherent stability of everyone else's mind except our own.

The mind wanders because that's what it has been trained to do. When I lived among the Yorùbá people of West Africa, I noticed the emphasis they placed on "home training," particularly in traditional households. A child who misbehaved while visiting outside the family—who failed to greet people properly or show kindness and respect for others—was immediately identified as the product of "bad home training." Elders would shake their heads and quietly repeat, "Bad home training, no home training." So it is with the mind—when we send it out to do something, it reveals its earlier training in distraction, in restless questing toward one fleeting pleasure after another. Since we've trained so vigorously and so long in the direction of distraction (for who knows how long, really?), why should we expect that, like the proverbial snowball rolling down a hill, it would suddenly change direction and roll back up?

So that's the bad news: training in distraction and restlessness has been going on for longer than we can remember, and the result of all that prior training in mental agitation stares us in the face every day. Why is this? As an old saying has it, "The chickens come home to roost." We've let our mind wander here and there while forcing it to pay only enough attention to get the job done—to drive a car or move from one Web site to another or listen to an important announcement.

The good news is: since the mind has been trained to go, it can be trained to stay. The suggestion of the core teachings from the meditative tradition is that our training in stability will certainly succeed, in part because the discipline of meditation accords with the fundamentally stable nature of the mind. Our training is going with the grain of the wood— even if several layers of accumulated dust make that grain hard to see at first, at times almost invisible. Nevertheless, we can gently wipe the dust away to reveal the basically good wood underneath.

The underground stream that flows toward awakening is strong, a very deep river indeed. It may not always be visible on the surface, where it can sometimes seem that everything is tending toward grasping, selfishness, indifference, aggression. As Suzuki Roshi says repeatedly, "The point we emphasize is strong confidence in our original nature." This confidence is born from genuine experience. It has been tempered by alternating fire and water, the slow process of heating and cooling on the meditative journey. It's not mere theory or just a matter of belief or unquestioning faith. Meditation is a real testing ground for the truth of our own basic goodness.

THE VALUE OF LOOKING FORWARD

I recommend preceding each session of meditation practice with a brief period of contemplation: thinking over what you're about to do, why you want to do it (the benefits of a stable, clear mind for oneself and others), and how you will go about training your mind in the way of this practice. I have met meditators who keep a copy of a favorite, inspiring book on mindfulness-awareness near their sitting place—and before each sitting session they read to themselves for a few moments, maybe just a few paragraphs to get ready—somewhat like doing a few preliminary stretches before beginning an exercise routine. Both the body and the mind appreciate this gentle, slow, deliberate on-ramp approach to practice. Traditionally this is called "contemplating the view" of meditation—and yes, it's highly recommended. As a meditator in Alabama said to me recently, "It's like jumping onto the horse and riding off in some direction, without first taking a moment to settle into the saddle and decide where we're going."

And still, you might ask: "Do I really have to go through this whole rigmarole each time before I practice? Can't I just do it?"

Of course, it's up to you. If you've already got your spurs on and are ready to go, why not proceed? Being ready to go, however, includes knowing where you're headed. As a famous Tibetan song of meditation reminds us, "just doing it" without a view of where we're going leads to blindly wandering—as though we circled endlessly around a supermarket, up and down the aisles, uncertain about what we're shopping for: fruits and vegetables? fish? bread? What was it again? Any practice needs a sense of direction and purpose.

Thinking over the view of meditation is like having an ally—it's a valuable aid and support to the practice. It's giving yourself a little extra help for the journey ahead. But if you prefer just to set out, that's fine, too. (It is possible to discover the view in the practice.) This is a supremely pragmatic tradition: everything is a matter of finding what actually works.

Sometimes our practice may grow slack. We lose interest, thinking that we're not having the right meditation experiences: "When am I going to start having all those experiences of unconditional peace and joy they talk about in the texts?" "When is my meditation going to evolve so that I'm more like Pema Chödrön?" Sakyong Mipham insightfully notes that often what happens is that we run out of *reasons* for meditating. Like a car running out of gas, we need more fuel to keep going. Our motivation dries up, and the journey stalls. Contemplating the view before practicing is like checking the fuel gauge and replenishing our motivation.

Sometimes I begin by just thinking over the meaning of the words "mindfulness of body." One could just sit with those words, recalling what one has read and heard about meditation. Say it a few times: "mindfulness of body, the body of mindfulness." Then, let the words fall away and rest in contemplation. That's a good beginning. It clarifies and focuses one's intention.

HOW WILL I KNOW WHEN MY BODY AND MIND ARE SYNCHRONIZED?

We monitor our practice as we go along—not to judge it and give ourselves a gold medal or a harsh reprimand, but as an expression of fundamental curiosity about our minds and bodies, our lives altogether. There is a saying that even if the Buddha himself were one's personal meditation instructor, practice cannot bear fruit unless we engage self-awareness. Ultimately, we are the ones supervising our practice sessions;

we are the ones who know if we're sliding into lackadaisical looseness or gripping ourselves tensely.

Suzuki Roshi often counseled his Zen meditation students to sit with "no gaining idea." Trungpa Rinpoche taught similarly of a "journey without goal." But giving up a goal orientation—having too much of a gaining idea in our approach to meditation—doesn't mean ignoring the details of our daily experience in a kind of bland indifference: "Who cares? Whatever. Let's just keep going. Keep sitting. Seen one sitting session, you've seen them all." This isn't meditative equanimity; this is training in stupidity.

In contrast, checking in from time to time to see and feel what's going on with body and mind is part of approaching practice as an appreciative inquiry, looking into how it is in our very being now. It's not enough simply to repeat to ourselves how we were yesterday, or the last time we practiced. This need not be goal-oriented or judgmental. Fundamental appreciation and kindness toward ourselves are expressed by taking an interest, asking ourselves, from time to time, in a deepening process of gentle, inner inquiry: how's it going?

On the other hand, practicing meditation is a bit like learning to dance—there's no need to keep self-consciously monitoring your progress, checking to see if you're doing the right steps, once you're actually dancing. As the poet Rita Dove suggests, dancing is like taking flight—no need to keep watching your feet or looking down at the ground. Trungpa Rinpoche developed a striking analogy for the level of confidence we feel when we're sailing along with synchronized body and mind: it's like "riding on oneself and playing a flute at the same time." This image expresses a deep trust in which we are no longer watching ourselves to see how we're doing. Instead, the feeling is one of celebration, harmony, and natural ease—not so much finally conquering a difficult mountain range as gliding along with our bodies, with ourselves, as we are.

HOW IMPORTANT IS DAILY PRACTICE?

Many people find that they meditate for a few days—and then forget about it. A few more days, and then they forget about it again. Occasionally some may like to do longer periods on weekends, when the mind seems to settle more. The weekday sessions may seem to not really be getting anywhere.

Regular, consistent practice is better than large chunks with not much in between. Sakyong Mipham has likened irregular practice to a boa constrictor's approach to eating: long periods of nothing, nothing, and then attempting to swallow and digest huge chunks of meditation practice. This can lead to spiritual indigestion.

Of course, given all the ups and downs of our lives and the challenges of busy schedules—caring for a small child, working for a start-up company, getting further professional training—time for meditation can sometimes be a scarce commodity. At times in my own life, finding the opportunity for occasional meditation seemed like finding a green oasis in the vast desert of busy-ness and speed.

The main theme in regard to deciding how much to practice is consistency; but we're looking more toward the quality of regular practice as opposed to just logging in some time every day. I remember hearing Trungpa Rinpoche speak of "sandwiching one's life"—between a period of meditation in the morning and then another in the evening. Some teachers emphasize short sessions, many times—and the importance of selecting an appropriate time period that can be accomplished without leaving us feeling tired, defeated, and discouraged toward the end of a session. If our session usually ends on a note of despair about the whole process, we're less likely to get back to it soon. Training works best if we establish a regular rhythm and then increase our stamina in small increments. As it says repeatedly in that great Chinese wisdom-book the *I Ching,* "Perseverance furthers." If what works in your life is meditating once or twice a week, then do once or twice a week—consistently.

Here we are approaching meditation as a companion to one's life—all of one's life—sunny days, cloudy days, mist and fog, freezing rain, and radiant brilliance. If we practice just when things in life are going well—or just in times of crisis—we develop a lopsided sense of ourselves, both in and outside of meditation.

I practiced meditation for many years with an ideal of perfection dangling out before me, like a perfect carrot tempting the donkey to move. If I felt speedy or tired, I wouldn't practice—because it was embarrassing to face how very imperfect my mindfulness was on those days, how far I was from attaining that carrot. So, on those days when I felt foggy or scattered, somehow less than "crystal clear," I tended to skip meditating altogether. If we secretly suspect that our next session won't be as good as the last, we may similarly avoid practice. Through too much idealism about meditative achievement, we set ourselves up for failure and inevitable discouragement. Like rope entangling our feet, these high expectations trip us up, and we stumble.

Occasionally a person may think to themselves, "Well, my mind is so distracted, so restless, maybe this mindfulness-awareness meditation is just not meant for me." Yet meditation seems expressly designed for those of us with restless, agitated minds. It is the wild and untamed mind that needs mindfulness practice and stability. After all, if the mind had perfect stability already, what need for the meditative journey? If we're traveling and already in Buenos Aires, why would we need to take the train there? If we remember this, then the "mental weeds" of distracted mind become the inspiration for practice, the reason to take the journey. As Suzuki Roshi wisely says, these mind weeds, like fertilizing compost, can enrich the garden of our practice.

COMPLETENESS, NOT PERFECTION

Completeness, not perfection, is the aim here. "Completeness" means that we include all aspects of our being —body, emotions, happy and sad thoughts, yawns and tears—everything is welcome in the house of meditation. Without both our welcome and unwelcome inner guests, meditation would be incomplete, partial, a one-sided experience of who we really are.

Sometimes being awake is imagined as a state of spotless perfection—a completely smooth life of the mind with no awkward stumbles, ever. This is unrealistic. What is truly inspiring about the accomplished meditators we sometimes meet—from Japan, Tibet, and Korea, or from the Burmese and Thai traditions—is being in the presence of complete human beings, people at home with all aspects of their being. Remember the seminar title created by Sakyong Mipham that so well describes the aim and purpose of meditation: being human. That's the journey we're making—toward embracing ourselves as complete human beings.

SCHEDULING?

Questions about scheduling tips are similar to questions about effort, and the suggestion is the same: we need to find a middle way. Here the two extremes (in which we set ourselves up for discouragement and burnout) are a strict, gung ho approach to scheduling or, on the other hand, a casual, looser style. In the more militant approach to disciplining ourselves, we make ourselves practice every day, whether we are interested in it or not, whatever the seasons of our life and activities. In the other extreme, the approach is: if the sun is shining, and we happen to feel like a little meditation as a pleasing spice or garnish to our life, then we give it a try—until the cell phone rings. These approaches may work for some of us. But for many people, the high bar of "gonna do it every day, come what may, hell or high water," leads to a backlash—in which we decide that, well, maybe this sitting practice of meditation isn't really for us after all. (Whether we consciously come to such a decision or not, our actions—or inaction—reflect this feeling.) On the other hand, when we wait, somewhat passively, for moments of inspiration to invite us onto a chair or cushion, we sometimes end up waiting quite a few days, which become a few weeks, maybe months. We wake up one day surprised to find that we have left our meditation practice somewhere back there by the wayside.

The middle way approach is to aim for some regularity—but with no need to be militant with oneself. Find an attainable rhythm—every other day, or both days on the weekend and once midweek, for instance—and then stick to that for a while, until it becomes as regular and workable as brushing your teeth every day. Evaluate after a month or so and shift up or down according to the seasons of life and your changing appetite for meditation. If you want to lean into it more in the winter months, when your work schedule is less demanding, then make that change. If, to the contrary, winter turns out to be a time of unusually demanding obligations at work or at home, then adjust accordingly. In this way we respect both our own impulses and the changing

circumstances of our lives. This intelligent responsiveness is
the essence of meditative awareness.

THE POSTURE OF MEDITATION

Question: Why sit in a chair?
Answer: Why not? You sit in a chair ordinarily, don't you?
Q: Don't you need to sit in full lotus posture on the floor to
enter deep meditation and attain enlightenment?
A: If you are comfortable sitting on a cushion on the floor
(which probably took some training of your body), then that
is a fine way to continue. That's the sitting position that has
been used in Buddhist cultures. I notice that there is often
a reluctance to use chairs for meditation, as though it's not
really kosher. In *Meditation in Action,* Trungpa Rinpoche
reminds us that chairs are also traditional: "But for those
who find it difficult to sit cross-legged, sitting on a chair is
quite good, and, in fact, in Buddhist iconography the posture
of sitting on a chair is known as the Maitreya asana, so it is
quite acceptable. The important thing is to keep the back
straight so that there is no strain on the breathing."

Note the emphasis on practicality here—it's not just a matter of form for form's sake. The physical posture is upright
to support wakefulness and should be vertically aligned in
such a way that one's natural breathing is not constricted by a
cramped, hunched-over position. If you can accomplish these
goals of relaxed alertness in body and mind better by sitting in a chair, then please do so. Keep in mind the difference between what's important and what's a matter of merely
looking good, that is, appearing to be meditating while suffering through a distracting amount of discomfort. You could
also alternate between some time sitting in a chair and some
time on a cushion, gradually strengthening and developing

different muscles in both postures. As has been said, the most important thing is to do it.

BACK PAIN, KNEE PAIN, SHOULDER PAIN

If you have an injury in a particular area, it's good to seek professional attention for it. If you're under the care of a physician or health care practitioner, let them take a look at the way you're sitting and suggest changes as needed, given your particular physique and personal history. There are many contemporary physical learning and treatment modalities (bodywork) that can be very helpful with posture—including the Alexander Technique, Rosen work, the Feldenkrais practices, Aston-Patterning, Rolfing, and many others. Many of us find that regular practice of hatha yoga or qigong helps with "establishing a good seat" for sitting meditation.

If minor physical irritations and stiffness arise, that is to be expected, as in learning any new physical activity. If we take up the tango or salsa dancing and begin stretching or moving in unfamiliar ways, we usually feel it the next day. Standing or sitting still is, in this sense, a new movement, and the body needs time to learn this quiet little dance. Include the sensations—pleasant and unpleasant—as part of the mindfulness-of-body practice; notice the stiffness or soreness, and then move, rather than strain unnecessarily. Here as well we're looking for a middle way—neither being harsh with ourselves in some misguided attempt at stoic asceticism, nor indulging the slightest whim of restless energy. Give your body time to learn to enjoy the stillness of sitting.

As for other sensations that arise in the body during meditation—sometimes you get an itch, or the muscle in your calf twitches—lots of things happen in the body as we're sitting there. These are all signs that the body we're being mindful of is a living body—not a corpse. Therefore we can include any physical sensations that occur during practice as part of the mindfulness-of-body meditation. If an itching sensation arises, let bare attention notice that. This is a good overall guideline for meditation—include, include, include. If something is happening already, there is little point in denying it or trying to push it out of the field of awareness. Far better to acknowledge whatever feelings or sensations there are, and then continue following the unfolding golden thread of mindfulness of the body breathing.

WHAT'S ALL THIS ABOUT ENJOYMENT DURING MEDITATION?

You may have heard that spirituality was supposed to be about transcending both pain and pleasure. And I've encouraged you here to enjoy the ups and downs of the meditative journey. What's that about? Another question I often encounter goes like this: "I really like meditation when my mind stays still and seems quiet for a little while, but I don't like all the mental noise. I'm just being honest—I have strong likes and dislikes, preferences for one state over another, and that's what I feel about meditation—sometimes I like it, other times I think I should just get up and feed the dog or water the plants."

We are exploring the possibility of joy, a heartfelt fullness of experience, a well-being beyond the passing and momentary experiences of pleasure and pain. Meditation is an ideal place to cultivate inquisitiveness, to awaken curiosity about the changing landscape of emotional experience, since, as we sit there, we're bound to feel sometimes happy, sometimes sad, jealous, bored, excited, rested, sleepy, anxious, mellow, irritated, and at peace with ourselves and others. In short, we should expect to feel the whole spectrum of emotional life—which we'll turn to in a moment when we consider mindfulness of feelings.

Meditative joy is connected with "making friends with ourselves" in a more inclusive, whole-person sense. This is the joy that comes from embracing what some psychologists call our "shadow," as well as from embracing our brilliance. Whichever is our greater challenge—our gloriousness or our wretchedness—meditation includes the whole range of our being. The joy of including all of ourselves is an expression of this great freedom and spaciousness.

6 Welcoming

The Feeling of Mindfulness

AS I WRITE THIS, I'm living in New York's Hudson River valley. This scenic, forested area near the Catskill Mountains and Woodstock has many farms and orchards. It's harvesttime here now, so all along the country roads there are many signs: "Pumpkins for sale—You pick 'em" or "Black walnuts—Free for the picking." Please take a moment now to reflect on our own picking and gathering and harvesting, so far, of the ideas and perspectives we've already placed in our meditation teachings basket.

Recall, for example, the importance of approaching meditation as a completely natural activity, not unlike waking in the morning and falling asleep at night. How do we do that? We're not entirely sure—we just do it: we place ourselves in a suitable position and gently encourage nature to take its course. Lying down encourages sleep; getting out of bed and standing up rouses greater wakefulness. In the same way, bare attention—the heart of meditation—is natural to sentient beings, and we cultivate and grow our innate powers of mindfulness by training in meditating, engaging a regular discipline. That discipline involves, primarily, placing the innate attention on, first, the body—encouraging the inherent stability of mind. Now we will move on to include awareness of feelings as well.

As we sit, we notice feelings. Sometimes we wonder: did I have all these emotions before? As when we sit down and notice the presence of a surprising number of thoughts (who would have thought?), we may also notice more emotional weather than usual (who knew?). So much desire, jealousy, anger, sadness, fear! Particularly during longer, extended sitting periods—of a day, a week, or more—meditators often experience a vivid roller-coaster ride of feelings: in the morning, excitement and anticipation of an upcoming wedding or anniversary celebration; in the afternoon, a piercing memory of childhood friends and sweet-sour feelings about the places and people we grew up around; in the evening, sadness and lingering grief at the recent passing of a loved one. Like a brilliant rainbow, the heart contains all the tones and colors of the spectrum, the full range of felt personal experience.

"I'm not usually so emotional," meditators in intensive training sessions sometimes say—as though the shedding of tears were an occasion for mild confession. Women and men both sometimes comment—after crying during a sitting session that allowed some emotionally moving memory to float to the surface—"I don't know what's wrong with me." As my English friend Simon used to say, "Aye, there's the rub, isn't it?" These comments reveal the underlying sense, the unspoken assumption, that being vulnerable, showing emotion, or even sensing our feelings of tenderness is somehow wrong. It's as though we feel we should turn our unruly emotional life over to an inner Department of Corrections.

THE "WORKING WITH THE EMOTIONS" GROUP

Back in the San Francisco Bay area, I used to lead a course called "Working with the Emotions," based in part on the section bearing that same title from Trungpa Rinpoche's classic map of the path, *The Myth of Freedom and the Way of Meditation*. Once a week, course participants would gather in a circle, having closely read the chapters related to our topic and practiced sitting meditation in the intervening week. Early on in our dialogues, we acknowledged to each other a simple fact of our psychology: we were all keenly interested in learning to "work with" our emotions because we regarded feelings as problems to be solved—or dissolved. We were approaching our emotions as something to be fixed. Someone noted, with a small smile, that this word, "fixed," is the same word we use for spaying and neutering animals. Yes, another person chimed in: "Or for getting the brakes fixed on the car." I agreed: approaching feelings as requiring "fixing" suggests the need for repair—for removing something unnecessary or unwanted and adding to what is basically inadequate. All too often, we approach our emotional life with a "poverty mentality": Something is basically wrong with me. How can I fix it?

One of the members of our discussion group worked as an editor for a local magazine. Sally usually arrived slightly late to our evening meetings, often carrying bundles of page proofs and galleys from her still unfinished work at the office. One rainy, wintry evening, she was the first to speak: "It's like we're all trying to be editors of our emotions. We look ourselves over and decide what gets to stay and what has to go. We move from hairy first drafts to smoothly polished paragraphs by crossing out certain embarrassing grammatical mistakes and supplementing the weaker parts of the prose. When it comes to feelings and meditation, we're all desperately trying to edit ourselves for improvement!"

The group considered this in silence for a moment—and then Jim, a psychotherapist for many years, added: "Yes—it's like we're attempting a kind of psychological surgery. We want to get out the meditation scalpel and skillfully wield it to remove all these problematic feelings. When? Now, if not yesterday. I see people in my office every day who say, 'Doc, help me out here, I don't have time for all these feelings that are coming up.' It's like saying, 'In my life I don't have time for life.'"

This was exactly Trungpa Rinpoche's often-repeated point—we can use meditation, in a subtle twist, as a way of avoiding our emotions, tamping down intense feelings in the interest of getting back to the more spiritual zone of "mindfulness." Life presents itself to us—in the form of unexpectedly falling in love, having a disagreeable argument, longing for some change in our daily rut. Like a sudden wind, we feel an upsurge of jealousy at another's undeserved success. We regard these internal events as interruptions in our practice—we can't wait until they subside so that we can get back to our regular life!

We feel gusts of emotional energy and even strong physical sensations that go along with feelings of fear, passion, and anger. We begin meditation with an attitude of openness, welcoming whatever arises in body and mind. The twist, however, is when we set up a holy zone of nonfeeling (after all, it's sometimes taught that the dharma is "passionlessness," right?)—and then use our meditation as a vehicle to get swiftly to numbness, to anesthetize ourselves. This is meditation as manipulation.

Sally was keenly attuned to this particular spiritual twist. "Meditation," she said, "should be prolife, in the sense of leaning toward a more vivid experience of being alive, with all the sights, sounds, and colors of a full life—sweet times and sad, happy moments and sour. But lately I realize I've been using meditation to try and turn everything into a gray mush—as if that's the meaning of the middle way. Maybe it comes from staring too long at too many images of stone-carved buddhas—it's like I'm trying to use meditation to turn myself into an unfeeling rock. What was that old Simon and Garfunkel song called: 'I Am a Rock'? Well, that's not human wakefulness!"

After laughing along with the rest of us, she paused for a moment to catch her breath, and then continued: "I keep trying not to get too excited about anything—and then again not to get bummed out either. I end up trying to micromanage my emotional life to keep it in the safe zone of a lukewarm middle. It ends up being antilife in the dharmic disguise of opening to life as it is."

"Exactly," agreed Jim. "And then I end up feeling so frustrated with myself and my meditation that I'm not actually able to keep everything blurry and toned-down, mushy and gray like you said—that I still end up feeling really happy sometimes. My oldest daughter just gave birth last week—to twins! Or sometimes, meditation or not, I just feel really sad—my father has Alzheimer's, and each time I visit him, I can feel him slipping away."

Again we all paused—hang gliding for a moment in the silence to let Jim's comments sink in. Then Juanita—who worked in the small repertory theater company just down the street—spoke up in her forceful, animated way: "Yes, well, actually I mean, no! That's not it at all, at least that's not the main problem for me, stuffing things down, making them all shades of gray. Over the last few weeks I've realized that I've been trying to keep my emotions all stirred up—it's why I was initially interested in finding out more about a Tantric Buddhist tradition of meditation. But my friends all see me as just another drama queen—hungry and vampirishly searching for one entertaining story after another, only to find myself stuck in reruns hell."

We laughed, all of us feeling familiar with both extremes—tamping down intensity, in fear of letting loose a raging wildfire, or stirring up some emotional drama as soon as life tends toward the bland or boring.

One evening, after several weeks of watching this emotional-strategies ping-pong match play itself out in our little group, one of the participants suggested that we all declare a "moratorium on manipulation," particularly on trying to change or even "work with" our emotions.

"What's a moratorium?" asked someone not yet born when the national moratoriums of the Vietnam War era made this a common word. Picking up a handy dictionary, I read aloud: "Moratorium: the delay or stopping of some activity."

"That's it!" shouted Juanita and Sally both at once. "Let's just stop trying to fix our emotions—at least for a moment."

Jim was more sober and cautious, while trying to be careful not to offend anyone's feelings: "Hmm . . . I can see where repressing or acting out our emotions is, as they say, getting us nowhere fast. But where's the positive wisdom in this idea of a moratorium?"

As usual, Jim's skeptical question was my cue to step in: "It's a little like the title of Pema Chödrön's first book—do you remember it? It's called *The Wisdom of No Escape*. In a sense, we've all been trying to escape our emotional liveliness—either by repressing or acting out. Both approaches are a futile attempt to get out of what we're really feeling."

Jane, an accountant in a small firm with offices in our building, added, "Yes—and it's too late to escape from what we're already feeling!"

Jim nodded, in partial agreement, but I could see he was still not convinced. Even if he kept silent, the doubtful look on his face spoke volumes: "We should try doing nothing? For this I needed years of meditation?"

"Think of it like this, Jim," Sally offered in her most earnest, trying-to-be-helpful voice: "There's that great quote you're always reminding us of from the beginning of *Cutting Through* about struggle and freedom—what does it say? 'There is no need to struggle to be free; the absence of struggle is in itself freedom.' Think of what we're doing in this period of a moratorium as practicing nonstruggle, actually putting nonstruggle into practice and in a sense liberating ourselves from the constant struggle to make more or make less of our emotions. Get it?"

Hoisted on his own favorite wisdom-quote, Jim grinned agreement. And so our group entered into an experiment: we declared a one-week moratorium on manipulating our emotions. It is this same approach—the wisdom of nonstruggle and trusting basic sanity—that provides the ground for our next session. Here we'll explore mindfulness of feeling in sitting meditation.

SESSION 2 *Mindfulness of Feeling*

As we add the mindfulness of feeling to what we've already been cultivating—mindfulness of body—we need to retain that solid foundation from our first session as the basis for further exploration. Without that grounding in the body, our awareness of emotions tends to float away—like a kite suddenly snapping loose in a strong wind. Who knows where it will fly away to next?

LOOKING FORWARD

So—when we begin the actual exercise, we will first feel our standing or sitting body, the weight of the physical form as gravity pulls it toward the earth. The physical sensations of standing or sitting, tightness in certain muscles, little movements while breathing—just allow them to come along. When we are aware of our body, we awaken into the experience of being alive as a breathing, energized body. Any physical sensations in our body—an itch on the earlobe, the weight of the palms face down on the thighs—are included in the mindfulness of body. Each sensation is like a little event, a little "happening," and we're present as it happens in our body as part of the mindfulness journey. At first these sensations seem to propel us along the path. They act as reminders to be present, like gusts of wind in our sails. Then we realize that these feelings—a twitch of the muscle in the calf as the body relaxes or the caress of refreshing, cool air on our skin—are the path of mindfulness itself.

We are standing (or sitting actually) on a threshold—the seamless transition from mindfulness of body to mindfulness of feeling. Our sensations are usually pleasing, displeasing, or neutral for us: "I like the feeling, the simple sensation of breathing in and breathing out. There's a quiet strength and contentment in the sense of my body at rest. But I hate that 'pins and needles' feeling as my leg wakes up after falling asleep." Take note of the felt personal experience of sensation—are we enjoying the sensations in the body, appreciating the flow of energy around the body? Or are we bothered that these particular sensations are here now? Or are we just indifferent, neither pleased nor displeased? Notice. Mindfulness means noticing—and not avoiding—the different qualities, the shifting texture, of experience while we're sitting, and it means being willing to include these feelings and sensations and emotions in our practice.

Further—and this expresses the essential bravery of meditation—we're willing to touch the actual texture of whatever we're feeling. If we're having a sexual fantasy, remembering times of erotic fire with our beloved, we feel that. If we're remembering and still grieving a loved one who died long ago, we feel that. If we're having a revenge fantasy, imagining getting back at those who insulted us, we feel that. Whatever it is, we take the view that we're willing to touch it and feel the underlying texture, for as long as it lasts.

FEELING THE TEXTURE OF EMOTIONS

Touching velvet feels different from touching ice, which feels different from touching warm water, which feels different from the texture of a moist leaf after a rainstorm. Our emotions have a similarly elemental quality—sadness sometimes feels droopy and watery, enthusiasm about a new project or a promotion feels like a windswept fire. This is the mindfulness of feeling: both the willingness to allow these emotions into our practice and the fearlessness to feel them fully, thoroughly, completely.

Recall our previous exercise with mindful eating, paying attention to the tastes of a piece of fruit. We worked on clearly distinguishing "bare attention" to the taste of an orange from thoughts about a remembered orange. This same crucial difference applies here: mindfulness of feeling means placing bare attention on pleasing or unpleasant feelings—as nakedly and directly as we can.

In this case, the contrast is between feelings that are "all dressed up" with ideas and theories and the basic emotions themselves. If we become angry—a slow, simmering burn—at the long lines at the checkout counter of a crowded market on a Friday afternoon, we talk to ourselves about our anger—it's the store's fault for not hiring more staff; it's the greedy city planners for allowing too much sprawl, making for a hopelessly overcrowded city; it's the rude person in front of us who has—count 'em—twelve items in a "ten items or fewer" express line. This internal chatter attempts to justify the frustration we're feeling—as though we are saying to ourselves and our inner chorus of judges, "It's right that I feel this way. Faced with a similar situation, wouldn't you feel this way also? Wouldn't anyone? Yes—this feeling is completely justified!"

We discover mindfulness of feeling in, as the Rumi poem suggests, a field out beyond wrongdoing and rightdoing. Mindfulness has nothing to do with whether a feeling is "right" or not, justifiable or irrational. We identify the storyline about the emotion, the running commentary that accompanies the feeling: "I'm right, except, maybe . . . I'm wrong; it's her fault that . . . he shouldn't have . . . and then I wouldn't have had to . . . it's childish to get upset this way, damn it, why does this keep happening?" We distinguish between this storyline of internal mental chatter and the underlying energy of the feeling, the actual emotional texture. Then we lean into the feeling itself. That's mindfulness and insight: we're using bare attention to get as close to direct experience of our emotions as possible—and we're using our innate yet sharpened sense of intelligence to feel the difference between talking to ourselves about what's wrong with the situation and actually feeling our fear. We're attending to the bare truths of the heart as the basis for uncovering our innate emotional intelligence. This is our path to awakening the wisdom of the heart.

Fear often prevents us from fully experiencing life, from directly relating to our feelings. Often, when we self-reflect and examine our hidden assumptions, we find that we are habitually approaching emotions as a threat—whether we deal with that threat by trying to tone down our feelings, by keeping a tight grip on them (as with Sally and Jim in our discussion group), or (as Juanita admitted) by drumming up something dramatic for inner entertainment and distraction.

What is the opposite of a threat? Well, an ally—someone or something that adds to our wealth, that provides additional resources for the fuller and deeper experience of basic well-being. In the exercises that follow, let's flip the warding-off-emotions-as-threat mental model and instead sink into our sensations and feelings without commentary. Sometimes, as the saying goes, silence is golden. When we let go of the discursive running commentary that seeks in vain to imprison the flowing water of emotions, we discover an inner wellspring of pure gold: a spontaneous treasury of bright color and dramatic display, filled with the humor and the sadness, the laughter and the tears, of the heart.

■ EXERCISE: MINDFULNESS OF FEELING

1. Sit comfortably on a chair or cushion, as before. Take a few moments after you find a more-or-less comfortable seat to recall the previous teachings on meditation: What is mindfulness? Why are we practicing it? Where is it going? How will we get there? In this way, we are contemplating the meaning, the motivation, and the intended destination of practice.

2. Then, gently but definitely, place your bare attention in the body—beginning with a full scan of the body if this helps you focus. Settle into mindfulness of the whole body, and then include awareness of the breathing. Feel the sway, the rhythmic back-and-forth, of the out-breath and the in-breath, breathing in and breathing out. Rest in this mindfulness of body for at least five minutes—coming back again and again to the body breathing when the mind wanders.

3. After stabilizing this basic ground of meditation, begin to explore the mindfulness further by paying particular attention to any sensations in the body—feelings of the temperature of the air on your face and hands, tension or relaxation in the shoulders, the flat-bottomed earthiness of your seat on the chair or cushion. Feel these sensations, including them in the mindfulness meditation.

4. After a few more minutes of this, as a training exercise, deliberately bring up a pleasant feeling as a platform for placing the attention. Commenting on the mindfulness of feeling, the meditation master Thich Nhat Hanh says: "When

we hear someone praise us, we may have a pleasant feeling." Use this as an exercise in your sitting by deliberately calling up the warm and pleasurable feeling of being appreciated and praised. Then, once a pleasant feeling has arisen, rest the mindfulness there. Let the feeling arise, stay, and go.

5. Then, briefly return to the previous practice of mindfulness of body, again grounding yourself in stability. Rest in the mindfulness of body, returning to it again and again and staying there.

6. Now, again as an exercise, give rise to an unpleasant feeling. For example: when someone criticizes us, it's rarely enjoyable, so imagine being criticized and the feeling of discomfort associated with that. Rest the mindfulness on the painful feeling of being criticized. Again try to take note of the arising of the feeling, its presence as long as it lasts, and then its leaving.

7. After a few more minutes of this, again as an exercise, deliberately bring up an emotion as a platform for placing the attention. If there are strong lingering feelings from your day, use one of those. If no particular emotion comes to mind easily, use desire. Call to mind something that you want more of—a favorite food or beautiful music, for example—and then allow the feeling of wanting, of passion, to be present, as long as it lasts. Touch the experience of desire—the feeling of wanting to taste dark chocolate. Feel this feeling fully, as directly as possible, letting go, for the moment, of inner comments about desire (or chocolate) being "good for me" or not. Let the experience of wanting arise, stay, and then go.

8. Then, briefly return to the previous practice of mindfulness of body, again grounding yourself in stability. Rest in the mindfulness of body, returning to it again and again.

9. Now, again give rise to the feeling of pleasure at some sensation—delicious food or drink, a beautiful scene you have

enjoyed—and then deliberately arouse desire for more of this pleasing sensation. When desire is present, place mindfulness on the feeling in the body of wanting. Again try to take note of the arising of the feeling, its presence as long as it lasts, and then its passing.

10. After a few minutes of contacting the feeling of desire, resting mindfully in the texture of that feeling and letting it go, return to the mindfulness of the body breathing—again focusing on stability combined with openness to whatever arises on its own. Ordinarily, this is how we would join the mindfulness of body with feeling—resting primarily in the sensations of breathing, while including a light touch of awareness of colorful emotions as they arise, dwell, and go. If they arise again—then again apply mindfulness, directing bare attention to the immediate sensations and feelings, getting as "close to the bone" as possible. Doing this again and again—this is the practice of mindfulness of feeling.

LOOKING BACK

Now that we've been diving, coming back up to the surface, and then diving again into the heart of feeling, let's look back over our meditative journey thus far. We began with attention in the body, feeling gravity pulling on the weight of the body as we sit still in upright posture. Then we moved deeper into this felt sense of the body to feel the ebbs and flows of bodily sensation—the various itches, pulses, and streaming movements throughout the body's muscles, tendons, ligaments. If we sit down to meditate just before or just after a meal, we may hear a stomach growl. When we adjust our sitting position for comfort and ease—for instance, gently lowering and raising our chin when our neck has grown stiff—we feel a whole range of tiny, shifting sensations as we move. After all, remember, this body that we're being mindful of is a living, breathing body, not a corpse. All these feelings are "fuel for the flame" of mindfulness.

Feelings are also "grist for the mill," meaning we have found something that can be used, something helpful for what we're trying to do. Although strong feelings may initially throw us off, seeming to destabilize our practice with sudden upswings and downward swoops, we can bring all these to the path. Recall Suzuki Roshi's saying that eventually these "mind weeds" will enrich our practice, like rotting compost fertilizing a beautiful summer garden.

These feelings and our mindfulness are revealed as "not two"—it isn't that we stand outside ourselves, observing our feelings as from a distance, and apply mindfulness to these inner sensations. The feeling of love, of tenderness, of joy is mindfulness already. Once again, practice isn't adding anything but rather realizing the deep, flowing vitality already present in our being. Feelings are wakefulness.

Still—we may wonder (along with Miles Davis): "So what?" Having read about the practice and explored a related exercise, there are further questions: What's the point? What would be the fruit of realizing mindfulness of feeling?

Mindfulness of feeling allows us to develop an unconditional sense of well-being, a deep joy in being alive. At a recent retreat's meditation instruction interview, for instance, I talked to Annie, who had been practicing meditation for three years. We were talking about joy in this deeper sense. She said that recently she had a glimpse of what is meant in the meditation teachings by a less-conditioned sense of joy. "Meaning what?" I asked, curious to see where she was going with this.

"Well," she said, "it's like those dogs in the famous Russian experiments."

"You mean Pavlov's experiments in conditioning?"

"Yeah, Pavlovian conditioning. The dogs were trained and conditioned—those are sort of the same, right?—to expect food whenever they heard a bell sound. Eventually, just the sound of the bell would cause them to salivate."

"So?" I was still curious but beginning to feel impatient.

"Well—all the conditioned pleasures in my life are like that—when things go the way I want them to go, then I'm happy; I salivate at the right stimuli. When things don't go my way, I get upset—right on schedule. Sitting meditation is one of the few things I do where it isn't a matter of getting the right pleasurable things to happen. It isn't a matter of making anything in particular happen at all. Some days it's boring, some days it's calm and contented. So what? There's some kind of unconditioned being, a sense of fundamental well-being, whether it's sunny or not. This is the strongest sense of real inner freedom I've ever felt in my life."

"That is well said."

7 Fear and Abundance

Conversations about
Mindfulness of Feeling

HERE ARE SOME RESPONSES I'VE HEARD when teaching mindfulness of feeling. Maybe some of them will also sound familiar to you.

Question: I gotta tell you that this seems much more complicated than the basic mindfulness of body we were doing before. That seemed so simple; what a relief! As soon as the feelings and emotions and all sorts of psychological factors come in, my straightforward mindfulness goes right out the window.

Answer: Experiencing the richness of the realm of feeling can seem daunting, almost overwhelming, at first. Just when we were finally beginning to settle down and find some comfort and ease in the grounded simplicity of body-mindfulness, we discover that this ground is itself in motion: slowly it moves, and sometimes it even shakes! It's like one of those old science-fiction movies in which an intrepid band of space travelers finally finds a planet to land on, somewhere in the outer reaches of space. Happy to have found a place for even temporary landing, the travelers relax, only to gradually become more and more alarmed with the realization that the planet itself is alive and sentient, somehow aware of their presence.

Similarly, our mindfulness of feeling says to us: "Welcome home, traveler." This mindfulness is a vivid reminder that our bodies are not inert solids, static and dead. We've landed (through our mindfulness-of-body practice), and now we realize that this earth we've settled into is alive—teeming with crosscurrents and winds and streams and molten lava and even an occasional earthquake.

Q: So, I'm confused. Is this a whole other practice we're doing now, or is it just the same old mindfulness we've been doing all along?

A: In a sense, it is the same old mindfulness as before. It's just that now we're paying bare attention to our physical form and the myriad sensations arising and falling in it from moment to moment. There's no strict line marking the difference between attending to the body and, now, awareness of the feelings as well. This is an organic, gradual development, a seamless process—as we settle down on the stable ground of the body, naturally we feel the sensations and movements within the still form. We're attuning ourselves to the sparkling fountain of upsurges of life itself—in our body. As Trungpa Rinpoche used to say, it's like discovering "an old new world." This practice combines the old and the new, familiarity and surprises, both the known (welcome, home; yes, we live here in the house of the body) and the unknown (as Dorothy understates it in *The Wizard of Oz:* "I don't think we're in Kansas anymore").

It's true that mindfulness of feeling often seems more challenging than simple bodily awareness, particularly at first. But the real challenge would be trying to fend off feelings, sensations, and emotions—protecting our safely contained mindfulness practice from these "invaders," as though they were outside agitators. These are inside agitators!

Avoiding feelings in practice is impossible, anyway. As we open to ourselves, we discover the truly inclusive nature of mindfulness, awakening to all aspects of our being—physical, emotional, mental. Though we have an idea that these are separate, like discrete rooms in a house—the bedroom is over there, the kitchen is over here—in reality these realms are all part of one big dwelling place, our basic being and its expressions. As we are sometimes delighted to discover, the morning smells of breakfast cooking travel easily from kitchen to bedroom to basement—all over the house.

Experiencing the variety of sensations can be bewildering and exhilarating at once—like standing in a dazzling, multicolored garden of flowers in full bloom. We have no hope of bringing simple mindfulness to this explosion of color unless we remember the crucial distinction between naked, bare attention and conceptual *thoughts* about the flowers. If we get involved in a long chain of discursive thoughts, talking to ourselves about where these flowers came from, who planted them, were there flowers before these?—then we've drifted. We've left the main highway of simple mindfulness behind and gotten lost on one of the many convenient conceptual side roads.

This is not to say that, at another time, it wouldn't be very useful to know all the relevant botanical information about these flowers: Would they grow in another climate? Would they require a lot of watering? Can we plant nasturtiums near zinnias to the mutual benefit of both? Such information about our inner and outer gardens is useful, perhaps even vital—but in the practice of mindfulness, our goal is bare attention to the feelings themselves. As much as we can, we rest there.

When we become aware that we have drifted into a storyline—even a credible story about where this sadness or that anger came from—the instructions are to simply notice these thoughts about feelings and return to the felt perception of the body and its sensations. This is really the main point with the mindfulness of feeling. Remember this, and return to this way of approaching the meditation practice again and again.

Q: I feel like this is encouraging me to repress my emotions, and I don't want to do that. I already know what happens when I bottle things up for a long while—eventually it backfires, and I erupt. I bitterly remember one longtime meditator who kept insisting to me that my feelings were "empty," he said, just "thinking," that is, simply a combination of physical sensations and concepts about them—as if this weren't a concept as well! I felt that this was a rather diminished view of human emotions. Are you trying to get us not to feel so much?

A: Not at all. To the contrary, this mindfulness practice is leaning in the direction of feeling more. "More" in the sense of feeling without filters, without the extra padding of storylines. We're not using meditation to avoid the rich challenge of our inner life. Finally, we're taking the gloves off, at last! We're feeling more directly and nakedly, with our bare hands.

Many of the meditators I meet are already familiar with Trungpa Rinpoche's wonderful teaching on meditating with a light touch, with a sense of "touch and go." This key meditation instruction relates to your question. One meditator said that she understood this instruction this way: "'Touch' means that we don't avoid. We're willing to move close enough to have actual contact with whatever we're feeling, sensing, experiencing—pleasant or unpleasant, both uncomfortable and enjoyable feelings. On the other hand, 'go' means we don't try to hang on to a particular emotion of passion or jealousy or whatever, nursing it for all it's worth with extended violin accompaniment and layers upon layers of judgments and opinions about why we're feeling this way." *Let us do the touch and go.* That's it, in a nutshell—no exaggerating and no diminishing, just the tender opening to feelings precisely as they are.

Q: In the exercise you led us through, you used passion, wanting, desire as an emotion to rest the attention on mindfully. What about other feelings—fear or anger or irritability, or even just a dull gray feeling of "blah"? Sometimes I don't have any particularly dramatic feeling—just a kind of ho-hum sense of going along with my life.

A: The same instruction applies to any feeling. There's nothing special about desire—it's just easier, sometimes, to begin with passion; it's familiar and feels relatively safe for some of us. If you're feeling adventurous, you might take one of the other, more challenging emotions and deliberately include it in your mindfulness practice of a particular session. You might also work with including neutral, dull feelings.

If you do this, remember to begin by first establishing some groundedness in the body, and, after the exercise of sensing the arising and falling away of a feeling, return at the end to this basic ground of the practice, letting whatever arises come and go freely. In other words, always remember to drop the deliberate exercise and return to nonmanipulation. In our ordinary practice of sitting meditation, we simply include sensations and feelings as they come along—without any attempt to manipulate or to force a particular result. To approach the emotions with a sense of nonmanipulation—that's the essence of the mindfulness of feeling.

TOUCH AND GO

Training and Nature

Let's contemplate the practice instruction to tou
in relation to our twin themes of training and n. . in
a sense, touching the feeling is applying the discipline of
mindfulness. It's training ourselves to do something besides
the habitual pattern of talking to ourselves about what it is
we're feeling, about why we feel the way we feel, about what
others have done to make us feel this way. Touching involves
right effort, applying just enough exertion to accommodate
feelings of love or sensations of lust or our tender heart of
sadness—and to let those feelings be as they are.

Going, on the other hand, involves further trust in the fundamentally awake nature of mind. Mindfulness is natural—
it doesn't require any further nursing or effort—it's spontaneously present and clear. Confidence in this original nature
is expressed by letting go—once we've touched the feeling with bare attention, we don't have to try to staple our
mindfulness there. Many unskillful meditators try too hard,
overshooting the mark by applying too much exertion and
force—as though the goal were to glue the mind to its object.
Instead, the skillful approach is to simply touch and then let
go into natural mindfulness. Apply some effort—and then
trust, have confidence in basic goodness, the fundamental
healthiness of mind.

As Trungpa Rinpoche explains: "The object of awareness
is developed, and you focus your attention on it. But then, in
the same moment, you disown it and go on. What is needed
here is some sense of confidence, confidence that you do
not have to securely own your mind, but can tune into its
process spontaneously." This spontaneous process refers to
the natural wakefulness of mind—what is present already,
without extra effort. So we apply ourselves and then let go,

floating; we train and then rest, finding once again in our own experience the trustworthiness of the union of training and nature.

SURVIVAL, SCARCITY, ABUNDANCE

When strong emotions arise, they seem to threaten our very survival. Even though it's just a passing, intangible psychological event, we feel as though the presence of anger or jealousy calls our existence into question. At the very least, a wave of emotion raises the question: who's really in control here? Am I riding my emotions, or are they riding me? Am I sitting in the saddle—or are these things pounding on my head like the hoofbeats of wild horses? Because of this question of fundamental control, we experience heightened emotions as both exciting and threatening.

On the one hand, we are glad for the excitement of some colorful feelings—life would be a very dull affair indeed, if we always trundled along in a terminal gray zone, never falling in love or rejoicing in a good friend's promotion. Gathering to raise a glass in good cheer, we celebrate graduations, marriages, and the birth of a child, silver anniversaries and sixtieth birthdays. Emotions awaken us, perk us up, arousing a sense of movement and liveliness. Suddenly, something—it almost doesn't matter what—is happening! The novelist Toni Morrison once spoke of her wonder at her two sons; she noticed the way they seemed so enlivened by the sense of danger.

So, on the one hand we're grateful for the arrival of some emotional color. On the other hand, we're anxious that our emotions don't get out of hand, out of our control. Not long ago, in the waiting room of my dentist's office, I felt sympathy for the anxious young man fidgeting in the chair next to mine. Eventually, after our eyes met a couple of times, we both put down our magazines and began a conversation about the recent fortunes of our favorite baseball teams (the Mets and the Rockies). After a few moments, he confided that he cries sometimes when he visits the dentist—and worries that he's a "bad" patient for being unusually sensitive to pain. Where did we learn this curious ideal—that good patients are always in complete control of their feelings?

In everyday life—at the office, for instance, even alone in our cubicle—we feel the pressure of keeping a tight grip on our emotions. It's embarrassing to be revealed as addicted to rage, or stung by jealousy, nervously insecure, or tearfully sad. Like handling a pack of wild dogs only recently tamed, we are careful to keep these feelings on a tight leash. As in my Bay Area study group, we usually swing back and forth between anxiously trying to turn the volume down on our emotional music or, bored with too long a steady state, trying to turn it up, to pump up the volume.

Both these approaches reflect an attitude of basic scarcity. When we desperately try to control our emotions, the underlying assumption is that they are arising as threats to our stability. Strong emotions—not just fear, but certainly being afraid is an outstanding example—bring up the feeling, "Am I all right? Have I survived? Am I going to be OK?" We even say this to friends who are experiencing strong feelings of grief or sadness: "Are you all right?"

Even with strong desire—when we feel that we really want something or someone—the issue of survival is implied in our desperation: "Am I going to be all right if I don't get what I want?" All of this is related to an attitude of scarcity, lack, inadequacy—is there enough, is there going to be enough for me, my family, my company? The unconscious belief driving our anxiety is that there is, basically, a scarcity of well-being—there's only a little to go around, and we are afraid that we will be the ones left hungry, lost, unloved, and unfulfilled.

A mentality of wealth, on the other hand, of abundance, involves generously allowing our feelings to be as they are. For once we're not busily trying to manipulate them so that we'll feel better. Our basic well-being is not at stake; we're not under attack from our feelings. Instead we're starting from the experience—even if only a glimpse—that our nature is, fundamentally, already whole and in fact completely filled with well-being. Basically we are not in need of adding anything or taking anything away. Therefore, a mentality of wealth allows us to practice the mindfulness of feeling: we can afford to include the ups and downs of life as further expressions of a basic richness.

My friend Tony says that he first noticed a range of difference in how he relates to his feelings last year when his workload left him more fatigued than usual. "When I was well rested, when I'd had enough sleep, hadn't been overworking myself, I felt like I was running on a full tank of gas—little things didn't upset me so much. I felt like I could afford to let the other guy go first sometimes. But when it was near the end of the week, and I was getting exhausted, the smallest little thing could send me into a rage. For instance, there was a long line at the post office one afternoon, and by the time I got to the window I was fuming—'This is gonna make me late for my appointment with Barbara, dammit, and that will ruin everything!' Then, fuming and upset to begin with, when I finally got to the window and the clerk, I bought the wrong stamps and sent the package to the wrong address!

"It wasn't just that things didn't go my way. What I noticed was that my own negative feelings bothered me more and more. I realized at a certain point that mostly I was upset about being upset. I was angry at my own anger most of all. This was an important clue for me—it's not just my feelings, but my feeling about my feelings: that's where meditation allowed some shift to take place. Of course I still get irritated and upset—I still hate long lines; but I stopped beating myself up for being the way that I am, feeling the way that I feel."

MINDFULNESS OF FEAR

Lately, I've been contemplating this passage from the Dzogchen Ponlop: "The practice of the second foundation, mindfulness of feeling, is relating to our basic existence as samsaric beings. In the general Buddhist approach, 'feeling' refers to working with our basic fear, which is the fear of suffering, or the fear of fear. Actually, fear itself is not suffering, but the fear of fear is the most troubling presence in the realm of our feeling."

Several teachers have explored the rich connection between the mindfulness of feeling and fear. There is a saying in the Shambhala tradition: "Unless you know the nature of fear, you cannot experience fearlessness." The same insight is expressed in President Franklin Delano Roosevelt's famous saying, "The only thing we have to fear is fear itself." We are afraid of feeling fear. If instead we take fear as the dawning of wisdom, it provides a path to fearlessness. We step beyond it by being willing to step into and through it.

Whenever fear arises—either in a sudden wind of panic or a low-grade brooding anxiety, chronic worry and concern or a moment of outright terror—the approach of the feeling-mindfulness is to fully feel the fear, to move toward it rather than running away. The fire of fear is usually mixed with the smoke of explanations, abstract considerations that attempt to tame the fear through various storylines about the fear. These storylines move us away from feeling directly.

The healthiest way to be with fear is simply that—to be

the fear, rather than trying to solve it or successfully manipulate it from a distant vantage point. Approaching fear from a distance is like having a giant pair of chopsticks—fear is at the end of them, twenty-five feet away from us, and we keep trying to move the fear from kitchen counter to dining table and back again. No wonder it keeps spilling onto the floor! Instead, we could approach fear as a finger food—using the bare hand to pick it up directly, place it in the mouth, chew and swallow. This is similar to Trungpa Rinpoche's brief yet evocative description of inner process: "There are several stages in relating with the emotions: the stages of seeing, hearing, smelling, touching, and transmuting." The path of mindfulness follows a winding road of increasing intimacy.

UNCONDITIONAL WELL-BEING . . . AND BOREDOM

The path to the experience of basic well-being leads through boredom. Passing through the crucible of boredom is an essential part of any meditator's journey. Unless we are willing to experience boredom, we cannot discover unconditioned joy—not dependent on external entertainment.

Boredom in this deeper sense has to do with the addiction to constant inner entertainment—the compulsive replays and reruns of mental movies of the past and the projected future. Ordinarily we don't notice these inner dramas, since they are partly interrupted by external events that require at least some of our attention. We may daydream a bit as we drive, but the presence of red taillights ahead of us or an irritated driver's horn sounding behind us demands our attention.

Sitting quietly in meditation is the best research lab to observe the mind's behavior when it isn't being interrupted, called to order. Sitting quietly, we inquire into our experience: can we exit our mental multiplex cinema at will? Or do you find yourself moving from one inner movie to another, to another, a triple feature of memories and fantasies of last year, next year, the ups and downs of love and work and family recast in a seemingly endless tape loop? Is this really freely chosen or a chained-to-the-theater-seat, compulsive habit?

Meditation practice is based on a simple commitment—the commitment to being here, to being fully present in mind and body. We are only able to practice and strengthen mindfulness if we remember our intention—to be present. This motivation gives us some leverage to come back, to return to the experience of our bodies sitting and breathing. Without that clarity of intention, we become mental channel surfers—when we wake up from one fantasy we quickly change the channel (let's switch to "work anxiety" instead of "romance") and go right back to another series of distractions.

Mindfulness can only be strengthened if we are willing to let ourselves see through these inner fantasies—and the seemingly powerful emotions that fuel them. Desire, revenge, loneliness, anger, regret, pride at a promotion, shame at losing our job—there is no DVD store with a comparable range of juicy titles, custom-fit to our current taste in emotion-packed drama. Cultivating mindfulness depends on leaving some space, at least between one mental movie and the next.

Occasionally we discover that the fantasies have faded for a moment—or their entertainment value has declined to the point of near-zero fascination. Sometimes these can be melodramas based on materials from our childhood, and other times they can be excited dreams about next week's travel to Vancouver. One winter, snowed-in in Colorado, I remember sitting for a week's meditation retreat. Day after day after day, I listened to the replay of old memory tapes about a childhood bully I'd fought with throughout grade school. As with the longer dreams we often experience during a good night's sleep, these waking dreams can be surprisingly vivid—we remember exactly what the first person we fell in love with looked like, the smile and the tilt of the head. At first these are surprising: Why this? Why now? Then we lose interest in analyzing the origin and become simply bored with the repetitions of a recurrent memory. Eventually, whatever the content of our favorite current drama, we adopt the same open-door policy—everything is welcome to arise, and welcome to pass on. Experiencing boredom is the inner key to touch and go.

Note that it isn't the dramas themselves that need to be transformed or go away. The main change is in our emotional investment in the inner movies. Without that fascination on the part of the viewers (you guessed it, that's us!), the show can continue or not—it doesn't really matter. Our attention can still be loyal, staying much closer, to the body breathing. Emotional dramas may float through, but we don't hook on for another roller-coaster ride. A certain renunciation of entertainment arises with the feeling of "been there, done that." Even as we're allowing our feelings more room, greater openness and freedom, we're simultaneously more stable, grounded.

Question: I can see that. I can see that I have the choice, as I'm sitting in meditation, either to go on with another fantasy, once I'm aware that attention is no longer with the breathing (if in fact it ever was with the breathing in the first place), or to remember my intention to be present—at least for this half hour a day when I'm training myself. And I can see that that requires some willingness to put up with being bored—or at least the threat of being bored, the possibility of a moment of life without drama or entertainment. But what's all this got to do with discovering meditative well-being?

Answer: That discovery involves a deeper sense of boredom yet again. One retreat participant described it this way. I'm going to quote her at length because she evokes her relationship with cool boredom so well: "During this afternoon's session, I noticed that staying with my breathing was much easier than before. Sometimes I still had waves of emotion left over from last week's end-of-the-year deadlines at work, but I wasn't fighting with these—they showed up, lasted as long as they lasted, and then moved on. They weren't really taking me away from the breathing, from the mindfulness of body—so I guess they weren't really even distractions, right?

"This was quite a change from last year's retreat, when I was in the middle of breaking up with Jeff. Whenever I sat during those turbulent times, it was like tiny emotional explosions going off one after another—boom! . . . and then he said . . . boom! Why did I ever get involved with someone so emotionally closed off? Then another sharp pang of regret: boom! Why was I always the one to have to express the hurt feelings in the relationship? Why does this keep happening to me?

"But today there was no such struggle between strong waves of emotion and being present, where I find myself struggling to be present with the emotions—to keep my head above water. I was sitting, I was breathing, and I was paying attention to my body breathing and the feelings coming along—that was pretty much it. I was struggling with the sense of nothing happening, with the sense of no big deal. As I sat, it seemed that nothing, I mean really nothing special, was going on—at moments I almost felt that I was starving—though I'd had a good and ample lunch. Ordinarily, at a moment like this—a slight pause in the action of life—I would reach for my cell phone and start mentally composing funny text messages to one of my friends. Or I would have a snack—more tea or a piece of fruit, yes, an orange would be just the thing. Or I

ch for my iPod, or e-mail, or Google an old friend,
Facebook.

"Instead, I continued with the sitting discipline, just sitting there—slightly anxious for some unidentified next, next, next? Bored. Restless. Boredom became the object of meditation. I let go into boredom, into feeling bored, into the feeling that nothing was happening. I was alone and wishing something else was happening, but it wasn't, this was happening—just this empty wishing and the simple bare-minimum experience of sitting there.

"Then something in me surrendered to the empty-desert quality of sitting there. I relaxed and felt myself slide into enjoying the plain simplicity of sitting. It felt uncomplicated—and refreshing. I appreciated the feeling of nothing special happening rather than fighting it, constantly anxious for something more, like a spoiled brat demanding one more cartoon show. I realized that beyond the narrow bottleneck of our demand, there is a large fullness available to us.

"It reminded me of traveling once with my mother in the South. We stopped at a farmhouse to ask for directions, and they offered us water from their well. It was just plain water—served in a heavy tin cup—but it was delicious. For a moment, I felt my thirst for that water had finally been quenched—a thirst I hadn't even known I had.

"Relaxing into boredom and discovering the fullness of something so simple felt the same way. I thought of another analogy: when we're bored it's like being hungry and wandering up and down the aisles of a giant supermarket looking for something to eat. There are literally thousands of items to eat in a large market, but we keep insisting on this particular product—say a new brand of cookies—that they don't have. The feeling of boredom is as though we're starving—complaining that there's 'not enough'—when all around us is a sea of plenty. Boredom is our rejection of that plenty, our insistence on the one product that isn't there. Our demand for entertainment, for something dramatic to feed us, is just like that. When that relaxes—and the tight, narrow grip of insisting on what's not here releases—we discover a deeper well-being, not based on dramatic highs and lows, but equally willing to accommodate both."

IS IT ALWAYS SO EASY?

Question: Sometimes these dharma descriptions make it sound so easy—working with the emotions, developing "cool boredom" through mindfulness of feeling. Is it always so easy for you? Really? What about difficult feelings that won't go away, really uncomfortable feelings of despair or resentment, feelings of inadequacy and loss of confidence?

Answer: It's definitely not always easy; we should acknowledge that up front. Let's explore this question of ease—when is it easy, how could it become more easy or ease-filled? We might notice, for example, that we have the hidden assumption that meditation should be able to make uncomfortable feelings go away, mindfulness as a kind of spiritual disappearing act: "Now you see the uncomfortable feelings, now you don't!" We can imagine the slightly surreal ad on late-night television: "Have you been feeling uncomfortable or anxious lately about peak oil, avian flu, global warming? Just meditate daily and those feelings will go away! Twenty-five-hundred-year-old money-back guarantee!" This is unrealistic—and more in line with approaching meditation as a practice of successfully ignoring our feelings (and the challenging realities of the world around us)—than really waking up. If our wakefulness is going to be connected to living and working in communities, it's definitely going to involve getting closer to our emotions.

When we awaken, we see clearly our own feelings and the reality of where we are. The title of Pema Chödrön's collection *Comfortable with Uncertainty* says it well. It's not that we make ourselves comfortable by pretending that things are certain and secure, that all will go predictably well in our lives and the lives of our loved ones, from now on. (After September 11, 2001, it is difficult to imagine us lulling ourselves into such false security, but then again sometimes one response to difficult realities is to soothe ourselves by pretending that things are smoother than they are.) The path of meditation is not a matter of becoming comfortable with false certainty.

Change and groundlessness and uncertainty are realities—and we practice in order to rouse the courage to see things as they are—including sickness, aging, and death. We are awakening the bravery of becoming more at ease with what's real, including the reality of uncertainty. On this path, we discover the greater goodness of reality, of truth, of letting be. Meditation involves learning to stay without the promise that it will get easier, that it will all become more and more comfortable as days go by. The notion that each day will be easier than the last is a false promise our delusion makes to us.

So—let us bear witness to the dissolving of an illusion: the sense that it might be, could be, should always be easy to awaken to ourselves, to the facts of our lives. The hearty realism of meditation is inspiring—it's an honest human truth that it's not easy to bear feelings of grief and despair, of anger and jealousy. Feeling these "negative" emotions is uncomfortable. We might as well call this aspect of meditation practice "being mindful of uncomfortable feelings." The practice involves paying attention to sensations that we'd rather not have, bringing awareness to feelings we'd rather not notice, and then staying there—as long as they last.

In a sense we're learning to bear ourselves, to bear with the more difficult mountains and valleys in our emotional terrain. We're strengthening our ability to bear emotional discomfort. My friend Tony mentioned that, particularly when he was tired, he was easily frustrated and frequently lost his temper. Often we verbally lash out at others—the slow driver in front of us (the nerve of some people, to be on the road when we're late for work), the person lost in conversation on their cell phone in the checkout line (oblivious to the fact that now it's time to pay: hello?)—because we cannot bear our own feelings of irritation. We strike out as though it will relieve an inner pressure—as though we will feel better if we can let some steam off with an angry remark.

Actually, just the reverse is the case—the next time we are feeling irritable, we are even more likely to lash out in anger again, as though a deeper groove has now been established in the pattern of our behavior. We're literally training ourselves in a karmic pattern of dealing with irritation by lashing out. Being able to bear—to embrace with loving-kindness—our "negative" and uncomfortable feelings, is the only way to break the vicious cycle of reaction, acting out, feeling irritated again, reacting.

Question: You know, I agree that it's difficult to put up with—much less "make friends with"—certain deep, inner feelings: shame, guilt, embarrassment, feelings of unworthiness, of being blamed. What's puzzling is that sometimes even the so-called "positive" emotions, like love or joy—even these are frightening. In my effort to keep things sailing along on an even keel, I end up toning everything down—even the happy moments. What's up with that?

Answer: A fear of intensity. It's as though the sheer energetic heat of happiness or love might melt the conceptual net we've placed over everything, including ourselves and our loved ones. Some days, stepping outside my apartment after morning sitting, the world seems refreshed—washed clean as after a spring shower. This happens to the inner landscape as well—we approach ourselves and our feelings less habitually, with fresh directness.

Mindfulness means we're more willing to inquire into feelings of joy or irritation: what is this? We're not just having a knee-jerk reaction, attempting to banish or embellish a feeling. We're letting our basic inquisitiveness peer into sentiments we usually welcome and into emotionally uncomfortable moments as well. Inquisitiveness is bravery. In this case, curiosity nourishes and strengthens the cat!

Question: I've been spending a couple of minutes contemplating the teachings on meditation each day now, before I begin the actual session. I'm using the phrases from before: "mindfulness of body, the body of mindfulness; mindfulness of feeling, the feeling of mindfulness."

Answer: The words are a helpful reminder that mindfulness is not cold, abstract, purely cerebral, or woodenly neutral. The feeling of mindfulness is rich, golden, textured, velvety. Mindfulness comes in many flavors: sometimes it's like bittersweet chocolate and other times it's like sour lemons. This mindfulness of feeling is dynamic, windy, oceanic, and buttery.

Question: Still, I wonder . . . how do I actually do this? I'm sitting there, more or less minding my breathing, and a feeling of sadness about a relationship breakup last year comes up as well. What do I do with that?

Answer: It's more a matter of not doing than adding something extra. If you're noticing a feeling of sadness, then that's enough. Once again: remember that we're not trying to fix ourselves. Therefore, success in meditating consists of many skillful not-doings. Don't move away from your feelings by attempting to distract yourself. Don't dress the feelings up with colorful costumes, the various stories of self-justification or inwardly directed blame—"It's right that I feel this way" or "What's wrong with me that I feel this way (again)?" Let be, and, as the poet Wallace Stevens says, "Let be be finale of seem."

This not-doing, letting be, is a fundamentally nonaggressive approach to our experience. If anger arises, don't fight it—and likewise don't fight the feeling of wishing it would go away. Don't encourage it or indulge it—don't add to the feeling of anger by deliberately replaying the scenes of insult and vindictiveness. If desire arises, don't stoke the fires of passion by mentally recounting the many amazing wonders of the beloved. (There will be time later for writing love poems.) Don't engage either of these: repression or indulgence. Simply let be. For the moment at least, declare a moratorium on the deeply ingrained habit of wanting to manipulate, change, fix our emotions—by abandoning it. If impulses to get away or to manipulate our emotions arise—then, notice those impulses as well. If you're welcoming whatever arises and a thought emerges—"I don't want to welcome this"—then, welcome *that* thought. Remember to keep it simple: the goal is mindful presence.

8 Awareness of Mind's Flow

I LOVE THE MEDITATIVE JOURNEY. When I first moved to Colorado to teach at Naropa University, my students often told me stories of their favorite hiking and jogging trails. They spoke in vivid terms of the peace around a local lake or the rewards of climbing a hill for the awesome view of the valley below. The meditative journey is similar in many ways. It's a familiar route for many of us by now—like going out for another run on an enjoyable trail. Yet there are always surprises within the basic familiarity, always opportunities for discovering something new. An animal we'd not seen here before bounds away from our approaching form: was that really a coyote? Geese overhead loudly announcing their seasonal migration remind us of the cycle of the year. Meditation is a naturally unfolding process.

This book's journey into mindfulness began with attending to the body, continued with exploring feeling, and now expands to include awareness of the mind's activity and flow. The body is the aspect of our being that is visible to ourselves and others. Though I can see your form as you enter the room, no one—except for stage magicians—claims to be able to see thoughts. Moving from the mindfulness of body to feeling and now to mind is a natural progression, refining our awareness as we move from attending to the grosser aspects of being to the most subtle, flickering dimensions. It makes practical, organic sense to begin with the most obvious part of our being (the physical form) and then gradually to welcome the more subtle impulses of feeling and mental movement as well.

Training the bare attention to stay is a way of developing our natural wakefulness. Meditation practice is the gradual ripening of the seed of awareness, our innate potential for awakening. The discipline of meditation makes use of what we are naturally (body, energies, mind) as a sound basis for establishing mindfulness.

My teacher called this approach to meditation and the spiritual path "the skillful way," using the flowing patterns already moving through our lives to proceed further. The unskillful way is to reject what we are, what we have to work with, in a misguided attempt to improve ourselves: "Never mind paying attention to what I am now, I need to focus on what I can become!" This misses the crucial point: it's only through appreciative awareness of ourselves as we are that we are freed to become different. Let's look now at how this directly applies to continuing to build the house of meditation. First we will review the skillful approach to body and feelings and then go on to mind.

Many practitioners of mindfulness have said to me that, after many years of practice, they realized that they have been trying to meditate without a body. In a time in which millions have a daily practice of various forms of hatha yoga as part of their spiritual path, this may be surprising, but we inherit a culture that habitually separated the "higher" dimensions of spirit from the "lower" realm of the body. During one weeklong retreat, a participant expressed her insight into the persistence of this mind-body split: "I realized that I had been trying to make my body lighter and lighter, as though secretly I was trying to become a little angel with wings. (It must have been some kind of mental hangover from all those paintings of cherubim and seraphim I looked at as a child.) Even though my rational mind now rejected such images as childish, even dippy, secretly that was my image of a spiritual person—an angelic being serenely floating above it all.

"When the mindfulness-of-body instructions suggested that we use the weight of the body, pulled down to earth by the strong force of gravity, as a vital part of stabilizing the mind, I was at first surprised: isn't true spirituality about transcending the body, the earthly and the mundane? Then, thinking it over, suddenly I felt almost magically relieved of an impossible conundrum—how to become what I'm not? Finally, I could just be the body, this body that I am, with a particular weight and mass and shape—and this that I already am could be the basis for the path of meditation. I felt relieved—and grateful."

Many of us have looked down one day to discover that we have been trying to meditate as though we didn't have bodies, as though meditating were a purely mental pursuit, just a matter of the mind. We park our bodies in a particular shape, the sitting posture—and then we go on to the important main event, which has something to do with the thoughts. Even when we consciously correct this mistaken view, there is often a lingering unconscious feeling that to be truly spiritual is to be light enough to fly, to be utterly beyond earthly forces and gravity. Spirituality, in this mistaken view, is mainly a matter of transcending the body, freeing ourselves from our earthbound state.

Yet one of the ancient, sacred images handed down to us is of the Awakened One touching the ground, placing his hand on the earth as a witness to basic sanity. Therefore, an earthy, grounded, no-nonsense approach to the spiritual life asks: since we have a body, why not use it and its weight as part of grounding ourselves in the present? This is the practical wisdom of the skillful approach. Rather than struggling with the facts of life, we appreciate that the situations we find ourselves in are fundamentally in league with waking up. From this point of view, our life as embodied beings is not an obstacle on the path but an opportunity for graceful, wakeful embodiment.

In the same way, since we have feelings, why not use them as part of the path? This might be more skillful, a more direct path than waiting for the arrival of a time of complete detachment with no sensations, no emotions. Alongside those unconscious images of floating angels, the other hidden image we often carry with us into meditation practice is of a stone-carved buddha—with no feelings, no sensations, no emotional ups or downs. We hear teachings on equanimity and imagine that it means a kind of lukewarm, steady state, never excited, never saddened. This gives us a skewed picture of awakening as the movement toward a state of flat-lining, the spiritual equivalent of a constant dial tone. Yet the only time we will be constant in this dial-tone way will be when we are corpses. With this view, practicing meditation becomes a way of deadening our life force. Instead, in the skillful approach that Trungpa Rinpoche called "the mindfulness of life," we include the ebb and flow of pleasing and unpleasant sensations and all the liveliness of our feelings of fear and desire and irritation as part of the mindfulness meditation. The energetic eruptions that seem to interrupt our meditation are all signs of life itself happening. To vary a phrase: life is what happens to us as we go on planning on awakening tomorrow. The light touch of awareness kisses these lively sensations, welcoming them into the circle of meditative care. In this way, mindfulness of feeling becomes the basis of awakening our heart of compassion, the "big mind" that cares for all beings. Here is a golden thread linking the sitting practice of meditation with sharing and caring for others in community.

Now we are going to apply this same skillful approach to working with our minds, to including the blooming buzz of mental activity within our meditation practice. Once again we are healing splits in our being, both potential and existing separations. Just as mindfulness of body joins body and mind, so now mindfulness of mind unites awareness with the rushing stream of discursiveness and mental chatter. The result? When we heal the divisions within our experience (mind quarreling with body, feelings distant from mind), we experience the quiet inner strength of basic being, a house undivided, united in facing the challenges of life. Body and feeling, mind and heart are synchronized, working in harmony, mutually supportive and awake.

SESSION 3 *Mindfulness of Mind*

LOOKING FORWARD

Before we begin our mindfulness-of-mind exercises, take a moment to think over the general meaning of mindfulness, the purpose of meditation altogether, and this particular approach of skillfully joining our meditative training with the original, inborn nature of wakefulness. When we turn our focus directly to the practice of mindfulness of mind, the main point will be including the various states of mind we experience as we sit here. This means noticing the movement of the mind, the ongoing flow of the thinking process: thoughts followed by thoughts moving to more thoughts and then on to other thoughts. First we trained in bringing the attention into the body and resting it there. Then we expanded our awareness to include the rising and falling of feelings. Now we are going to train in bare attention to the thinking mind itself.

Sometimes our "sleepwalking" life is compared to having an illness. In that analogy, the meditation teacher is like a physician, and doing meditation is actually taking the recommended medicine. As with ingesting any medicine, there are possible side effects. Because we are engaged in training the mind to stay, to settle with the breathing body, we may sometimes look at these ongoing waves of thoughts rushing by as a threat. Regarding mental activity as a threat to mindfulness is a possible side effect of practicing mindfulness.

Sometimes when I sit down to meditate after a particularly busy day at work, I say to myself: "Here they come." Proliferating thoughts seem like bandits suddenly appearing on the horizon in a cowboy movie of the old West. At other times, particularly when I'm bored, thoughts appear as ever-present, beckoning seductions into distraction and entertainment: "Hey, look over here now—think about me, me, me!" From the point of view of maintaining our meditative discipline, some wariness seems well advised. As Oscar Wilde said, "I can resist everything except temptation." Similarly, because we are training the mind to stay still, to remain present, we may end up regarding any movement in the mind as a bad sign, a warning signal that we've diverged from the way of meditation. This would be the view of a "concentration meditation," where the aim is to stamp out any movement of the mind, to bring the mind to a complete halt, the state of unmoving stillness. Please take careful note that this concentration technique is not the approach we are taking to mindfulness of mind. Most definitely not.

Here, practicing mindfulness of mind means acknowledging the thoughts that pass through our minds—their movement, momentum, and speed. Are there a few thoughts that move through the mind slowly, like a meandering river? Are there seemingly thousands of thoughts in an erupting, gushing geyser? Noticing the thoughts, their movement and frequency and pace—that is the essence of attending to the mind.

As the great Tibetan meditation master Dakpo Rinpoche said: "Thoughts are a meditator's friend." This wise statement neatly reverses the view of defending our meditation from the attacks of distraction. We have seen that a possible side effect of vigorously applying "the medicine" of mindfulness-awareness practice is that we sometimes view our thoughts as seductive or hostile forces seeking to undermine our hard-won spiritual discipline. Instead, Dakpopa suggests regarding thoughts as allies to our practice, companions on the path. In fact, we cannot practice mindfulness of the mind's activity without the presence of thoughts; they are like fuel for the fire of mindfulness. Whether we're using oil, gas, or wood: how are we going to ignite the flame of mindfulness unless we have something to burn?

■ EXERCISE: MINDFULNESS OF MIND

1. Take the seated meditation posture. First bring attention to the body, feeling the feet on the floor, the legs, the flat bottom on the chair or cushion, the torso, shoulders, arms, hands, neck, head, and face. Take your time and relax any tension you discover along the way. Then feel the whole body at once, engaging mindfulness of the body sitting. Then, as a direct extension of that mindfulness of body, include the sensations of respiration, the body breathing in and breathing out, inhaling and exhaling. Rest the attention on the gentle, soothing, back-and-forth rhythm of the breathing.

If your attention wanders from the breathing to the sound of car horns and traffic outside or the sight of a yellow rose in your sitting room, acknowledge this wandering, and then gently return the attention to the body breathing. Mindfulness meditation is sometimes called the practice of recollection. This name for the practice reminds us: there is real power in remembering to stay with the breathing and to return to it.

2. Then, as you sit, as you breathe and pay attention to your breathing, also deliberately notice your thoughts. Make sure that your mindfulness includes some awareness of thinking. Are there only a few thoughts, darting here and there? Are there, on the other hand, so many thoughts proliferating so quickly that it would be impossible to count them, like the number of stars in the night sky? Notice.

Pay particular attention to the movement of the thoughts—is it fast, medium speed, or slow? A traditional image is that the mind may be filled with many thoughts rushing along like a steep mountain waterfall. Another image is that the thoughts may flow along slowly, like a gentle, steady river. It isn't that one of these is better than the other; the point of mindfulness of mind is to notice the movement of mental activity however it is—fast, slow, or alternating between the two. The main instruction is to rouse an alert awareness of the mind in motion. In the same way that we initially brought mindfulness to bear on the taste of an orange, now we are bringing bare attention to discursive thinking.

Continue with your meditation practice for a few minutes, making sure that you include whatever sensations and thoughts arise, while continuing to steady the main body of your mindfulness by resting it on the breathing. The mindfulness of breathing is like a bright silver cord running through the entire length of a maze. Simple boredom or amazing things, all sorts of ups and downs, may occur, but we include whatever happens on the firm, wide platform of the grounded mindfulness of the body breathing.

■ EXERCISE: MINDFULNESS-AWARENESS

Meditating on mindfulness of mind is sometimes called mindfulness-awareness practice. We train in stabilizing mindfulness, which brings more ability to listen and work with a sustained focus in the rest of our lives. The simple exercise that follows will sharpen our awareness of our state of mind.

1. Sit, as usual, but then ask yourself after a few minutes of stabilizing, "What is the mind like when it is with the breathing?" This question asks us to look carefully and then describe what we see. This looking is more a matter of bare attention than thinking about the qualities of mind. This is a very important difference: as before, the aim is to *notice,* as nakedly as you can, without additives or filters, the qualities of the resting mind. Is it like a still pool of water? Is it like a cloudy sky? What is it like?

Note also that the aim isn't to evaluate the relative worthiness or unworthiness, the goodness or unwholesomeness, of a particular state. The question that sharpens the focus of our knowing awareness is, What is the mind like when it is more or less still? The question isn't, is it a good mind or a bad mind? Instead, ask, what are the qualities and characteristics of the resting mind? Rather than talking to yourself about these qualities—where they came from, how long they might stay—just look as directly as possible to see the resting mind's texture and character: is it soupy, lumpy, smooth, solid like a mountain, foggy?

2. Then, include some awareness of the mind when it is not with the breathing—ask yourself, and again look to discover the answer: "What is the mind like when it is moving, when it is not resting with the body breathing?" Notice that, in order to do this part of the exercise, we require some

period when the mind has moved away from the object of meditation, that is, when it is not with the breathing. Usually a two- or three-minute period provides more than enough time for inquiring into the movement of mind, but if you need longer to have some experience of wandering mind, take as long as you need. Again, notice—in the same non-judgmental yet inquisitive way as before—the qualities of the mind when it is not with the breathing.

It would be very easy here to slip into further discursiveness, talking to ourselves about our inner dialogues. In meditation, we often find ourselves engaged in an inner conversation about our mental state. "Why is my mind so restless today? Why am I still thinking about that? I thought I was over him already! Why do I even care so much what she did? What's wrong with me today?" This inner critic or voice of judgment comments incessantly on our various attitudes and states of mind: "That's good, now you're being really mindful. Pretty good. Maybe; maybe, try it again now. Nope, that was terrible—you didn't do that well at all, you schmuck. You're hopeless at this meditation stuff." The mindfulness-of-mind exercise, however, invites us to notice the qualities of discursive mind—without further comment. What is speedy mind like? What is lethargic mind like? However it is, that's it. Experiencing the mind, as it is, however it is, moving or still—that's the point of this exercise.

■ EXERCISE: INNER MENTAL STATES

As a final mindfulness-of-mind exercise, first establish your mindfulness in the body by means of the breathing. Then let go of the breath as the object of meditation and place the attention directly on the mind's own activity. Traleg Kyabgon describes this practice: "Having become accustomed to using the breath as an aid to establishing mindfulness, we can take a further step and turn our attention to our inner mental states as the focus of meditation." Now, moving entirely away from the notion of thoughts and feelings as distractions from meditation, make whatever thoughts are arising the main focus of your mindfulness. Bring bare attention to your mind's activity and stay with whatever occurs. If nothing occurs, rest simply. If something occurs—thoughts of passion or anger or jealousy—notice them. Whatever occurs in the realm of the mind, simply notice it and let it be as it is, without trying to make more or less of it.

LOOKING BACK

Mindfulness of mind is both a specific meditative discipline and a natural outcome of practice. Earlier we spoke of meditation as developmental, an organic process of gradually including more and more of what we are under the wide umbrella of awareness—first our bodies, then feelings, thoughts, and emotions. Step by step we settle into an ongoing, relaxed alertness, an awakened sensing and sensitivity to our physical and mental being.

Before, when we contemplated the usual "sleepwalking" state, we noticed that it has a certain momentum—the accumulated power of habit. We discovered that we're well-trained—almost too well-trained—in grasping and distraction. Now, having engaged the "countertraining" in mindful presence and well-being, we notice and appreciate the momentum of awareness as well. As the Dzogchen Ponlop says: "Once you have developed the discipline of mindfulness, awareness is simply the continuity of that mindfulness."

The continuity of this alertness is both the product of our training—we've cultivated a grounded attention that gradually expands—and a natural state. We discover that, without any extra effort to "make ourselves more aware," we're simply alert and awake to what's happening with us, in our body and mind, naturally. So mindfulness of mind is both the organic result of our mindfulness training thus far, its fruition, and the radiant expression of our inherently wakeful nature. As Trungpa Rinpoche describes the gradual development of meditation: "A quality of expansive awareness develops through mindfulness of body—a sense of being settled and of therefore being able to afford to open out." With mindfulness of mind we are simultaneously appreciating the harvest of our discipline and celebrating spontaneous wakefulness. Right meditation has a rich aroma that comes directly from the kitchen of awareness, a joyful union of exertion and celebration.

The ninth Karmapa, an outstanding sixteenth-century Tibetan meditation master, wrote of a "reverse meditation," in which we recognize thoughts as they occur and regard them as friends. This "reverses" the tendency to regard thoughts as distractions from the main focus; now the thoughts themselves are the main focus. Mindfulness-of-mind practice, then, is a further step on the path of making friends with ourselves. This is the heart of awareness practice: making friends with our entire being as a stepping-stone to embracing our world. The openness that we extend to ourselves in formal sitting practice continues in our off-the-cushion life as well. The aim is to meet others with that same grounded-yet-welcoming spirit. The sitting practice of meditation reintroduces us to a common ground of basic sanity we share with others.

9 Seeing beyond Hope and Fear

*Conversations on
Mindfulness of Mind*

THE FOLLOWING ARE EXCERPTS from conversations I've had with meditation practitioners during retreats.

Question: I've been thinking about the inevitable frustration of trying to "meditate without a body." Still, there's a lot of emphasis in the Buddhist meditative tradition on the essential importance of mind—and the mindfulness of mind seems to be a part of that. Why is so much importance attached to mind?

Answer: You're entirely correct—from the earliest teachings of the Buddha to the present day, all the meditation masters emphasize that the key to our experience of life is our state of mind. If we have the state of mind or attitude of a heavy tank—to use one of Trungpa Rinpoche's favorite early examples—then we will tend to roll through life practicing "the tank technique," ignoring much of what's said or done around us, just thoughtlessly pressing ahead with our own agenda. Whatever anyone else's suggestions or objections, the tanks (that's us again) just keep rolling along. If, on the other hand, our state of mind becomes more open, receptive, spacious, and appreciative, we rediscover the richness and intelligence and wisdom of life and those around us.

My friend Tony says that sometimes he can't believe that it's the same life that he's having now as he had two years ago. Looked at from the outside, it's certainly the same: he's in the same job, same house, same relationship. Yet, two years ago it felt like a hellish prison he was stuck in for "what seemed like forever." (This emotion-based exaggeration of time [forever?] is a sign that the mind is, well, exaggerating—emphasizing the negative, distorting our memory of how long this particular frustration has been going on or will last.) Now he says that he often feels grateful to his partner, his coworkers, even his boss at work.

What could have made such a difference? Could it really be that everything *external* has changed so much in a mere twenty-something months? Or is it that his state of mind has shifted and relaxed and expanded, so that he's not fighting with himself and those around him quite so much in a desperate attempt to finally get to "the good life"? He has, to his surprise, found a "good-enough life" already staring him in the face. Mind is the key to that shift.

If we are dissatisfied and want to understand the frustrating experiences we're having now, we can begin looking at our own state of mind. What's our attitude, what's our outlook on life, and what are the hidden assumptions secretly driving our states of mind? Mindfulness of mind opens the door into this deeper self-knowledge.

In classical Buddhism, mind is also the root of all our behavior. From our thoughts and attitudes follows our speech, and from what we say follow our actions in the world. Therefore, as the eighth-century Indian meditation master Shantideva repeatedly urges, we should pay careful attention to our state of mind. Just as we wouldn't place anything dirty or polluted in our eyes (we know that could easily lead to infection), we should also care for the basic sanity of our minds; the mind can become polluted as well, festering with old resentments, feverish with insatiable craving. Unskillful actions—a harsh comment that discourages a good friend, an angry e-mail fired off in a thoughtless outburst that we soon regret—all flow from a cluttered, chaotic, and reaction-based mind. Simplifying our lives for sustainability, finding harmony and elegance wherever we are, begins with simplifying our minds.

CLEARING OUT THE MENTAL CLUTTER

It's as though our e-mail inbox has been left unattended for years—now it's filled to the brim and overflowing with spam, with letters from family and loved ones, with job offers and "we regret to inform you" letters about the death of old friends. It's difficult to clearly see which of these letters is worth answering. What of this really matters to us? Is any of it urgent? It's like a basically beautiful flower garden, left unattended for several summers, so it's no surprise that it's crowded now and almost choking on its own growth. Mindfulness meditation allows us gradually to clear away some of the mental clutter and overgrown weeds, just by shining the bright light of awareness onto our own consciousness, cultivating our own inner garden.

Question: I understood a bit of what you were saying about the skillful approach—using what we are, what we have already as the basis, rather than always chasing after another, better basis—somehow always elsewhere and elsewhen. I can work with this some in terms of body (I've got a pretty good body anyway) and some in terms of physical sensations (usually not that big a deal). But mind! Sometimes it feels like I'm just being overwhelmed by thoughts. What then?

Answer: Yes, well, good. Sounds like you've definitely discovered the "waterfall" of discursive thoughts.

Q: Yeah, I can also relate to that—except that sometimes it starts to feel like I'm getting all wet, know what I mean?

A: Yes, and what is it that notices the volume and intensity of your thoughts?

Q: Awareness?

A: Yes—mindfulness of mind means that you are noticing, aware of, the torrential downpour of thinking. Is it always like that?

Q: Well, no, of course not, but when it is, how do I stop it?

A: Why would you want to stop it?

Q [*laughing*]: So that I can be more mindful?

A: Occasionally someone in a meditation retreat will say to me, "I'm not sure this meditation is right for me— I'm having so many thoughts!" But those of us with wild and distracted minds are precisely the ones most in need of mindfulness training. If the mind were already calmly abiding, why would we need a sitting meditation discipline to tame it?

Whenever we notice the wildness of mind—or its lethargy for that matter—we have two options. Noticing the flood of thoughts can be a time of discouragement, despairing of either the practice or ourselves as practitioners: "Look at all these (negative) thoughts I'm still having." Or, this moment of bare attention can be an opportunity for appreciating the fact that we've noticed our states of mind, whether speedy, sluggish, excited, or bored. We can celebrate discovering the jewel of noticing.

Question: Here's my story. It's not so much that I've become aware of thoughts, or of myself thinking, thinking, thinking. It's more that I've noticed that so often I'm talking to myself in a harsh way. I'm sure that if someone from the outside could see the way I treat myself on the inside, they'd say, "Hey! Lighten up, don't be so hard on that guy!"

Answer: Yes, Pema Chödrön mentions that Trungpa Rinpoche instructed her to pay attention to the tone of voice with which one says "thinking." Is it a negative slap—"thinking!"—like someone angrily swatting a fly? Is it a dreary drone—"thinking"—like "oh, there you are again"? It's almost impossible to practice mindfulness of mind without also cultivating loving-kindness toward oneself—one's good thoughts, bad thoughts, the silly and the sublime. So—noticing habits of harshness is the beginning of the path to gentleness.

Q: Yeah, but what if this inner mean streak doesn't go away?

A: Having a harsh inner critic is a little like adopting a sharp-toothed tiger as a household pet. The basic instruction is the same—don't indulge it, but also don't fight it. Clearly, adding aggression to aggression just makes us even tenser. So, the suggested guidelines are: don't feed it every time it growls (the food bill will be enormous, and it will only demand more as it grows fat and arrogant), but also don't repress it (it will only descend into an even more foul temper, glancing at us from time to time with a look that says, "You talking to me? You trying to get rid of me? Better think again, my friend.").

Q: Well—is it that I'm being too tight with myself? I mean, in terms of practicing the technique and the Buddha's instructions about "not too tight, not too loose." Am I the kind of person who automatically hears that as "not too loose, not too loose"?

A: Well, probably you know yourself much better than I do. But we need to tread carefully here—being harsh with oneself is not the same as tightening up the technique, paying more attention to being precise, leaning into the details. If you notice that you're simply "hanging out" daydreaming in the meditation posture and calling that "meditation," then it's definitely time for "right tightening." That is being kind to yourself. On the other hand, there is a skillful time for "right loosening" as well. When we trust in our originally wakeful nature, we realize that we don't need to overexert ourselves, the way impatient Americans traveling abroad sometimes yell to make themselves understood. This doesn't improve the communication.

Question: I continue to feel that there's something lacking in my meditation. There's just something missing. When I read all the stories of the great meditators of the past—women and men who attained enlightenment in one life-time, I'm truly inspired. But when I return to my own practice, settling down on the old cushion for another session with body, breathing, and mind—it's depressing. It's like watching stale reruns. There's no juice.

Answer: And this feeling of something missing, of a fundamental lack—ever felt that way before or is it just coming up with meditation?

Q: Are you kidding? I've felt this way most of my life—somehow nothing is ever quite enough. Whatever is happening, whatever situation I'm in, it's never quite good enough, just not really satisfying

A: Sounds like it's time to make friends with this pattern as well, don't you think? Otherwise we reject it as unsatisfactory and go on searching, seeking, craving. Mindfulness has a quiet dignity—it's there even in the posture. We're not just flopping down for another boring session of inner reruns, our own private televised version of "Nick at Nite." Just taking the posture of meditation, sitting up, arouses energy and confidence. It's a gesture of bravery, a silent proclamation of fearlessness: we commit ourselves to working with any state of mind that arises—sadness and excitement, boredom and joy, fear and desire. They're all welcome, fundamentally welcome.

Question: You mentioned noticing our thoughts in terms of their movement and speed, but what about our psychological patterns? Tara Bennett-Goleman writes about the persistence of self-defeating mental "schemas," and Ken McLeod analyzes many "reactive patterns." Wouldn't mindfulness of mind include paying attention to my own particular habits of mind?

Answer: Yes, it certainly would. Bare attention to our thoughts leads directly into noticing patterns of mind: our recurrent jealousy or puffed-up pridefulness, hungry insecurity or chronic feeling of being victimized. Mindfulness means gradually becoming more and more familiar with the building blocks we use daily to construct our inner prisons—the states of mind that entrap us. When Trungpa Rinpoche taught on the traditional Buddhist six realms of being—hungry ghosts, jealous gods, and so forth—he called them "six styles of imprisonment." Becoming familiar with our habitual styles of imprisoning ourselves is the first step in dismantling these inner prisons altogether. Mindfulness and insight are our chief tools for freeing ourselves. Then our innate wisdom and compassion compel us to help free others as well. Natural wakefulness becomes a strong motive force that moves us toward helping others.

Q: Sort of a "meditators of the world, unite! You have only your chains to lose" approach?

A: You said it.

Q: I notice that many of my thoughts are often about one subject in particular—me!

A: Yes, Sakyong Mipham has taught extensively about our obsession with "the me plan." The beginning of the realization of what's called "egolessness"—the absence of a permanent, independent self—is becoming aware of our sense of self. Me, I, myself—what is the real meaning of these words?

Q: Well—what's striking is that the vast majority of my thoughts are about how I'll look to others. Will they think I'm pretty? Am I smart enough or will people treat me as a "dumb blonde"? Will they respect me, admire me, love me? It's like a litany: "they, they, they; me, me, me." Many of my thoughts are about puffing myself up in some way so that I'll look good to others.

A: Yes, mindfulness of mind is the basis of investigating our sense of self—as well as our concern with self-image. Notice the frequency of thoughts along the lines of: "How am I appearing to others?" There's a basic insecurity at work here—I depend on others to affirm and validate me, as though I secretly fear that, without them, I'm nothing. There may be an insightful intelligence wrapped in the guise of that fear. You know the saying: "Fear is the beginning of wisdom"?

Q: Something like that. It's like there's an imaginary audience for my life, even when I'm alone. Even when I'm sitting, I notice that I'm talking to this audience in my head, saying stuff like "I'm doing pretty good now, right?" And stuff like that goes on all the time. It's like I'm always looking at myself in a mirror of others' opinions about me, commenting on me and how I'm doing, how I'm meditating or whatever.

A: Yes, this is a form of what's sometimes called "the watcher." We watch ourselves—not the same as mindfulness at all!—and self-consciously *comment* on how we're doing: "That's good, that's better, that was terrible, oh, that was even worse, now, almost, now, now, that's great! Do it again." Particularly during meditation, we can sense that this running internal commentary on how we're doing is unnecessary. We don't need to ride ourselves, telling our minds to be mindful. At a certain point we simply have confidence that we are mindful. We trust that we are being mindfulness itself, with no separation between doing and being. The path to this "wordless confidence" is there when we remember that mindfulness of mind is just bare attention—with no added commentary on mind, feeling, or the body breathing.

Q: And if I find that there's still this unnecessary internal voice commenting on what's happening, how I'm doing?

A: Then just notice that, bring bare attention to the judging or commenting mind, the watcher, with no further comment. Sound familiar?

Q: So, what I'm understanding so far is that through mindfulness of mind, we're noticing our states of mind— happy, sad, worried, excited, whatever.

A: Yes, that's right.

Q: Well, that's all well and good, but lately what I've been realizing is that I never particularly wanted to notice my mind. That's part of why I've always kept myself so busy, so occupied with doing something, talking about something. Even when I came to meditation, I wanted some way to change my mind, not to get to know it as it is.

A: And what do you think that's about?

Q: Hmmm . . . fear. It's some kind of a fear of being alone with my own mind. Like when I was a kid I was always frightened by the silence, so I usually kept up some kind of chatter, talking to myself even when I was alone. So now this is related somehow, a fear of paying attention to mind.

A: It's good that you recognize it as fear. Sometimes we fool ourselves, blaming the external situation for what's going on inside, or we mistake anxious avoidance for passion, feeling that if we stir something up we will be more alive, more loved. Often, what's driving that impulse is a simple inability to sit quietly with ourselves, body, speech, and mind. So, yes, one of the states of mind we might become aware of during mindfulness-of-mind practice is fear—we might be mindful of the feeling of fear in the body, the slightly panicky thoughts racing through the mind. Being willing to experience that is another expression of the bravery of sitting meditation practice. We are strengthening our courage—our ability to stay with ourselves and our experience even when it's uncomfortable—by facing fear directly.

LOOKING THROUGH OUR MENTAL WINDOWS

Question: In a sense these various states of mind—whether angry or fearful or romantic—are like windows we're looking through. Life looks a little rosier, almost golden, when we're in love. On the other hand, when we're discouraged it's like the words from a bleak poem: "The world is ugly, and the people are sad." Our various states are like looking from a particular perspective, a certain angle of vision that either emphasizes all the golden highlights or dwells on all the warts.

Answer: Yes. You could say that an important aspect of mindfulness of mind is that it allows us to look at our mental windows and not just through them. As Ken McLeod says: "When you are completely identified with a pattern, the projected world of the pattern is taken to be the way things are." When we look out a tinted window, we can easily forget that it's partly the perspective of the viewer (rather than what's simply out there) that shows things in a certain light. Mindfulness of mind grants us a potential freedom to experience even the same old people and places in a fresh, new way. This is a powerful shift.

Q: I'm starting to appreciate the discipline of the mindfulness of mind—it takes exertion to stick with it when I'd rather run away. I feel like I'm finally discovering the true meaning of doing "inner work." But what about what you said earlier, about this mindfulness as a natural result of going along with the practice altogether, a kind of organic fruition that spontaneously blossoms, sometimes to our surprise. That doesn't sound like it's just a matter of hard work. What's that about?

A: It has to do with recognizing an inborn, natural alertness. Recognize and appreciate that. You discover a clarity, a knowing quality of mind, that you definitely did not produce.

WHAT IS IT THAT KNOWS?

Sometimes we notice our awareness in terms of distraction. Let's say it's the middle of winter, yet we've been daydreaming about summer in the country—the warm air, the brilliant sun and fluffy clouds. Suddenly we remember—meditation! "Oh yes, mindfulness, back to the breathing." Yet we often overlook a jewel here: what is it that knows we were fantasizing about summer and warmth, rather than imagining a ski trip and snow and crisp, cold air? Somehow we know, we're aware of, the "distracted mind"—it's not just a blank in the tape of memory. So there is a sense in which a mindfulness of our minds takes place spontaneously, without any effort on our parts. Having exerted ourselves in our discipline, we relax and discover an effortless quality to meditating. This is worth exploring, rather than dismissing it as worthless or useless out of a misplaced, spiritual work ethic—as though "if I don't struggle for it, it's not worth anything!" Consider the wisdom buried in old sayings: "Some of the best things in life are free."

Question: Even in an evening meditation session where I'm mostly distracted, where my mind seems to flit here and there, from a memory of my third-grade teacher's gray hair to the music at my father's funeral, at the end of the session, if you asked me where my mind had been, I could say— yep, back in third-grade art class, trying to sketch Ms. Lilly's wavy hair. Or, I'm remembering the cemetery, the long walk to the graveyard. It isn't like I wouldn't know at all what I'd been experiencing or that I would think I had been imagining pizza when in fact it was pesto. Is that what you mean about awareness knowing distraction—that even when we seem to be "absent" there's some kind of "presence" in that as well?

Answer: Yes, something like that. This is difficult to talk about. There do seem to be times when we are just lost in a fantasy completely; we've forgotten it's winter and where we are and what we're doing. Waking up from such a vivid day-dream can be a bit of a shock: oh! Suddenly we're back. Yet there are also moments when there is awareness of memories arising—as memories—and awareness of them going. Then other thoughts and fantasies arise—as thoughts and fantasies—and then they too take their bows and exit. In one text the arising and ceasing of thoughts is said to be like writing on water. So much for our usual image of a long train of discursive thoughts!

There's something spacious and accommodating that allows whatever comes to come and whatever goes to go. This natural alertness is much more continuous than the simple on-and-off quality of bare attention to the body breathing. It welcomes whatever arises, and so it has sometimes been called "choiceless awareness." As Sakyong Mipham says of our fundamental nature: "This basic goodness is a quality of complete wholesomeness. It includes everything."

10 Opening the Doors of Perception

Mindfulness of the Sense Fields

THUS FAR, our approach to training in natural meditation has been similar to the environmentalist slogan, "Recycling for sustainability." Rather than going on a spiritual shopping trip, searching for shiny, new products specially designed to increase our meditative stability, we have begun by using what we have already. We have and are bodies, we have and are feelings, and our minds are lively with thoughts—and perceptions. Trungpa Rinpoche notes that, in some religious traditions, "sense perceptions are regarded as problematic, because they arouse worldly desires." As we train in natural wakefulness, however, our approach to the senses is accepting these perceptions as invitations into further mindfulness, as open doorways into a larger environmental awareness.

This basically sane approach to working with ourselves is actually as old as the Buddha. If we recall the famous life story, after periods of sensual indulgence in the palace and then a harsh life as a wandering ascetic, Shakyamuni discovered and proclaimed a middle way. Now we are following that venerable tradition by including sense perceptions in our practice—neither indulging them in elaborate fantasies of further fulfillment nor fearfully avoiding and repressing them. We are practicing mindfulness of the senses as a middle way.

We see, hear, smell, taste, and touch every day. The senses are part of our natural condition, our ordinary state. Why would we reject this fundamental, human inheritance when we turn to the spiritual path? Once again, true spirituality invites a deeper appreciation of our basic state of being. Seeing, hearing, tasting and the rest are intrinsic parts of the wealth of being human.

The key to practicing mindfulness of the senses is developing an attitude that neither accepts nor rejects. There is a well-known story of the Indian Buddhist saint Tilopa, instructing his most famous student, Naropa: "O Naropa, we are not imprisoned by the world of the senses—it is our attachment that binds us." How so? Attachment is grasping after sense pleasures—if only there were more, a little more, once again, when can I have more, more, more? Another taste, another glimpse of such beauty, more pleasing sounds. Searching for more sensual fulfillment, we wander in the foggy valley of hope. The traditional phrase "grasping and fixated" and the contemporary paradigm of addiction describe our relationship to romantic fantasy, food, the thrill of exciting sports. Our grasping minds are stuck to that, hooked. Disappointed and wounded when this grasping inevitably fails (for even if momentarily sated, we soon turn toward hoping for the next pleasure), we embrace a personal period of "prohibition": "I'm swearing off _____ for a while. It's pointless and futile anyway, don't you think?" This rejecting of the colors and flavors of our world arises from an attitude of fear. We are anxious, worried about being seduced (again) and disappointed (again) by sense pleasures. The three exercises that follow are best approached without hope (for the future) or fear (of the past). The essence of mindfulness is nowness: This present sight. This ringing sound. Now, the taste of this strawberry. Here, mindfulness means attention to the sensations of the moment.

■ EXERCISE A: MINDFULNESS OF THE SENSE FIELDS—LOOKING AT THE OBJECT

1. Place a flower, a smooth stone, or a piece of wood (your choice) in front of your meditation seat. Begin as before, first establishing the foundation of your practice with the mindfulness of body. Then place your attention on the object before you. Notice its shape and color. When your mind wanders elsewhere, gently return it to the visual form. Do this for at least five minutes.

2. To conclude this exercise, take a few moments to look around the room—with the same mindful inquisitiveness you brought to the stone. Look at the shapes and colors of objects in your room—chairs, tables, doorknobs, lamps, rugs. Notice both the words you say to yourself about the objects ("That's my favorite lamp") and the wordless, bare attention to the forms themselves. Notice.

■ EXERCISE B: MINDFULNESS OF THE SENSE FIELDS—LISTENING TO THE OBJECT

Repeat the previous exercise, using sound as the object of attention. If you have a small gong, you can use it to produce a tone. Gently tapping a cup or glass of water will also work. Notice the sound, paying attention to it one-pointedly. If your mind wanders, return as before. Again, conclude with a more open focus: listen. Listen to the sound of cars and buses and motorcycles going by, to birds singing, to voices inside your home or outside in the street. Listen to whatever sounds are around you, resting in the silences between them. Welcome these sounds, and let them go—without further commentary ("I hate that sound, I wish there were more birdsongs"). If there is internal dialogue about the sounds, then listen to that as well. Return again and again to welcoming and noticing whatever sounds arise.

■ EXERCISE C: MINDFULNESS OF THE SENSE FIELDS—WASHING YOUR HANDS

This final exercise engages the mindfulness of seeing, hearing, and touching all together. Each time you wash your hands during the day—from wake-up until bedtime—be mindful of the sound of the water splashing on your hands, the sight and feel of the soap, the temperature of the liquid running over your palms. Let go of any previous occupations during the time of the hand washing—a meeting or conversation you've just left, a phone call or e-mail message waiting back at your desk. Be present with the simple activity of washing, with the variety of sights, sounds, and textures at play here.

MINDFULNESS OF THE SENSES

After you've done the previous exercises, you may have some questions similar to the ones addressed in the conversations that follow.

Question: I've done the mindfulness-of-the-senses exercises a few times now, and I don't see what the big deal is. So, I'm mindfully washing my hands; I've washed my hands thousands of times in my life. So what?

Answer: There is no big deal. As Suzuki Roshi often phrased it, there's a quality of "nothing special." We are not looking for an extraordinary or peak experience. Mindfulness is ordinary.

Q: Then why do it? What's the point? What am I supposed to be getting out of this?

A: Let's start with what you *are* getting out of it. What was your experience of practicing mindfulness of sense perceptions while washing your hands?

Q: My experience? Well, first I turned on the tap, and—

A: Whoa, partner! What did you actually notice during that?

Q: Umm, I felt the slightly cold, hard metal on my right hand as I twisted the knob.

A: Good; much better. Then what? In specific details. Remember the saying, "The devil is in the details"? Mindfulness is precise attention to details.

Q: As I waited for the water to warm up, I noticed many impatient thoughts, like, "Hurry up already!" I also noticed the rushing sound of the water, sort of a continuing "whoosh-sh-sh" sound. Then I saw the lime-green soap and felt its slippery texture as I held it in my hands.

A: Excellent. Please continue.

Q: And then—just like I've done a thousand times before, I lathered my hands with the soap, put the soap away, held them under the water and washed them off. Oh—I also remember noticing a slight perfume smell of the scented soap. But most of all I remember thinking, "What am I supposed to be getting out of this?" I did the exercise in the morning before work and then in the rest room at work, by which time it was already pretty boring.

A: Good, good. Lots of juicy details—sense perceptions are always specific. It's not an abstract, generic sound or sight but this whooshing now, this lime-green in the present. And boredom is a key entryway here.

Q: Entryway? Into what?

A: Into sensing what's actually happening—the present experience of washing the hands, eating an apple, crossing the street.

Q: Yeah—but it's still the same old world.

A: Yes, you're right; it's not, suddenly and magically, a different bathroom sink or a different job or street. Pine Street is still Pine Street. And yet it is a different experience of that same old world. Trungpa Rinpoche compared it to experiencing an "old new world." Unless we are willing to taste some boredom with the fantasies of being entertained by something special, unless these expectations wear out a bit, the doorway into this "old new world" remains firmly shut. Sometimes we are willing to stay with the meditative journey through the desert of hot boredom turning to an oasis of cool boredom. Stepping into the house of meditation, we settle down and open out. All the doors swing wide open, and the windows let in a cool, fresh breeze.

Question: Wow, I mean, I for one really like this mindfulness of the senses stuff. As they used to say back in the day, this is groovy. Why didn't we do this from the very beginning? It's much more fun than just sitting there following the breathing. Why not start this way?

Answer: Remember our middle way approach to meditation? One extreme would be closing our eyes to the sacredness of the colors and forms around us: blue, black, red, yellow, green. From the enthusiasm in your question, sounds like you don't have to worry too much about that one. The other extreme is using sense perceptions for entertainment— a natural movie? A heightened peak experience? We begin each time with the mindfulness of body to first establish a home ground. Then we move through boredom with discursive thoughts and fantasies, wearing out some of our habitual fascination with emotional dramas: "He did WHAT? She's moving WHERE?" Without that grounding and bore-dom, meditating on the senses becomes just another way to entertain ourselves, the ultimate DVD. We want to include but not indulge—this is another example of "not too tight, not too loose."

SUPER-SOUNDS, SUPER-SMELLS, SUPER-FEELINGS

Last summer, a small group of us were mindfully exploring sense perceptions together in the mountains of northern Col-orado. Nature was in full display, a tumbling waterfall of color: blue, green, white, yellow, red. The experience was inspir-ing, joyful, surprising—like discovering hidden wealth that we never knew we had. Maria reminded us that in Spanish there's an expression of delight—*que rico!*—which literally translates as "how rich!" This richness of the sensory world is not a mat-ter of money or the size of an investment portfolio. It's free—freely given and only received in spacious freedom.

During that retreat, someone read aloud from *Sham-bhala: The Sacred Path of the Warrior,* the provocative pas-sage where Trungpa Rinpoche says, "Your sense faculties give you access to possibilities of deeper perception. Beyond ordinary perception, there is super-sound, super-smell and super-feeling existing in your state of being. These can only be experienced by training yourself in the depth of medita-tion practice, which clarifies any confusion or cloudiness and brings out the precision, sharpness and wisdom of per-ception—the nowness of your world."

After a moment's silence while we contemplated this, someone piped up in appreciation: "That is well said, beau-tifully well said." Then someone else agreed but wondered:

"Yeah, sure, but what's this about super-sounds and super-sights? Sounds kinda trippy."

Well, as Trungpa Rinpoche explains, ordinarily we narrow the meaning of perceptions. Lime-green soap reminds me of washing up this morning, red lights mean stop—and that's all. Sights, sounds, and the rest are limited to their conceptual meaning. But there's so much more to the actual experience of red and green than "stop" and "go." Again we're like Pavlov's dogs, for whom the sound of a bell ringing only meant food in the scheme of their conditioning. As Trungpa Rinpoche continues: "We fit what we see into a comfortable or familiar scheme." These super-senses he speaks of are like the sense-fields unleashed, no longer confined in tiny conceptual cages. A larger expansive world opens through awareness of the senses. He concludes: "It is possible to go beyond personal interpretation to let vastness into our hearts through the medium of perception."

Much of our lives, we're just skimming along the dull surface of things, but mindfulness of the senses offers a deeper, richer connection to life and the world around us. A deeper experience of light and color, of pulse and sound, is often celebrated in the arts. Isn't this part of the reason we love music, paintings, dance? From this perspective, the art of meditation has a deep affinity with all the arts. Like the arts, meditation is a celebration of being alive.

11 Awakening from the Nightmare of Materialism

The materialistic outlook dominates everywhere.
—Vidyadhara Chögyam Trungpa Rinpoche

THE APPROACH TO THE SPIRITUAL PATH outlined here emphasizes the naturalness of awakening. Training in embodied presence with open hearts and minds is a gentle practice of encouraging the unfolding of our innate potential. Now we need to turn to directly considering the nightmare of materialism from which we are awakening—and the manner in which wakefulness can be expressed in strong connections to others.

For some years now, I've been leading weekend, weeklong, and monthlong meditation retreats in North America. I also do solitary meditation retreats whenever I can. It was during one of these retreats that the idea arose of writing a book on "natural wakefulness"—a phrase used by my first meditation teacher—and the nightmare of materialism. When I mentioned this idea to friends in my meditation community, they sometimes asked, "What do you mean by 'the nightmare of materialism'? Are you just talking about 'getting and spending,' the avalanche of rampant consumerism?"

Dictionaries usually emphasize the conventional understanding of "materialism," where it means "an attitude concerned almost exclusively with wealth and material possessions." This is the sense in which we sometimes say: "Did you notice that Gene is getting really materialistic lately? Maybe it's his new friends at work, but all he talks about lately is his flat-screen TV and his new car." In this narrow sense, materialism is often contrasted with an ethical or spiritual concern, the sense that there are "higher" values that matter more than "worldly" things. As the bumper sticker reminds us: "The best things in life are not things."

Right now, however, we are considering a wider, much more far-ranging materialism that includes spiritual ideas and practices, possibly even meditation itself. What makes these part of materialism? How is it that even meditation and spirituality could be practiced materialistically? We need to explore three key questions: first, what is the materialistic *outlook?* Then, we can turn to look at how materialism is *practiced,* actually carried out daily in our activities. Finally, we need to contemplate the *result* of this broader materialism in our communities and culture today.

Materialism in this wider sense has been with us all along, throughout our meditative journey. This isn't a new topic. In our contemplation of mindfulness-awareness meditation, we began with appreciating our precious natural resources—body, feelings, and mind. Yet we've also noticed the habitual tendency to grasp and fixate on our bodies, emotions, thoughts, and sense perceptions. This grasping and fixation is the action of materialism.

THE FEELING THAT
SOMETHING IS MISSING

The root of materialism is the sense that we are, in some fundamental way, inadequate. We feel, secretly, that there is something basic missing. Something is originally wrong with us—and the obvious solution to this inner lack is to get something, someone or some things, from outside to fill this inner gap. We need to explore how much of our usual sense of being "all right" is tied to receiving something or someone from outside. Often, I discover an underlying feeling: "I am all right because of what's out there; this is OK because of that." Let's move slowly while examining this habit of looking outside for inner well-being.

Remember as well that nothing along this journey needs to be simply accepted and believed. Our approach throughout the exercises in this book has been to take these teachings and test them, see if they're true. How? By looking more closely at the truth of our own experience. Our meditation practice has been one such testing ground.

Now, how would we test whether we are truly comfortable with ourselves, resting in a state of well-being that is not dependent on something coming to us from outside? Simple: spend some time, even a few moments, without any entertainment or reinforcement from outside. Spend a few moments in silence. Yes, this means take five minutes and put down this book, turn off the blogs and MP3s, leave the cell phone off. Also, leave the meditation project "off" for this test period as well; in other words, don't meditate! Just sit quietly for a few moments, and take note of your experience. Many of us soon notice an anxious itch to be talking to someone (wonder what Mary's doing these days?), to write another e-mail (why hasn't he responded already?), even to be back at work (gotta finish that project). This restlessness and uncomfortableness are experiential symptoms of the inner sense of lack, of the feeling of not being enough.

Many of the behaviors in our so-called soft addictions are telltale signs of this basic anxiety: overeating, staying up late watching television, wasting hours online or with mail-order catalogs. Try this, as an experiment: notice the withdrawal symptoms when you let go of just one of your favorite, habitual ways of distracting yourself for even an hour or an afternoon.

What are we distracting ourselves from? From our experience of ourselves, the plain bare experience of ourselves as we are without add-ons. As Trungpa Rinpoche has written: "We must face the fact that fear is lurking in our lives, always, in everything we do." Test this out: is it true? Do you have some core feeling of shame or lack, of loss and emptiness? Some spiritual psychologists say that it's as though there are inner holes we're constantly trying to fill with things from outside.

How did this habit of distracting ourselves start? Once again, from training. We've been trained, very well trained, in the outlook and practices of materialism, almost from birth. Look at the earlier and earlier ages at which children, infants really, are being hooked onto the consumerist treadmill. Many of our children grow up hearing thousands of messages daily, urging them to buy this doll, play that video game, hurry and get this new electronic toy. I remember being struck recently, going out for dinner in a shopping mall with friends and their young children in Chicago, at the repeated cries around us of "Mommy, Daddy, buy me this, buy me that!"

I told this story at a Shambhala Training program in Boulder, Colorado. Someone raised a hand to ask, "What's wrong with that? Why shouldn't we enjoy the latest technological toys? And surely love and companionship are among the great pleasures of life, right?" This leads us to a key point, absolutely central. It's not that the things themselves are a problem. The problem is our toxic fixation on something outside to make us feel better about ourselves. That fixation becomes the source of greed, aggression, fear, jealousy, lying, and deception. What do I have to do to get it? If I lose the object of my romantic quest, I'm left spinning, lost. If I don't get the next golden carrot dangled before me, I feel flattened into self-hatred. Then we decide to buckle down and really get serious: if anyone interferes with me getting who or what I want (what I feel I need to be happy), look out! The repercussions range from domestic abuse to warfare. As the bumper sticker asks: "How did our oil get underneath their sand?"

THE THREE LORDS OF MATERIALISM

Back in the early 1970s, Trungpa Rinpoche articulated, with his usual penetrating brilliance, three main realms in which we practice the materialistic outlook. Using traditional Tibetan metaphors, he discussed these realms by referring to them as the Lord of Form, the Lord of Speech, and the Lord of Mind. When we were contemplating mindfulness, we also noticed the fixation on ideas of body, our many concepts of emotions, and the multiple theories we hold about mind and its activities. Now we are turning our attention to larger cultural patterns of solidifying.

The Lord of Form

The Lord of Form includes our relationship to our bodies as well as to the "body," or form, of the world around us. As Trungpa Rinpoche explained, "The Lord of Form refers to the neurotic pursuit of physical comfort, security and pleasure . . . our preoccupation with manipulating physical surroundings." Be careful here: it's not the physical world itself, but the psychological clinging that so quickly turns things sour, polluted, stagnant. It is this clinging attitude that drives us, motivates us, to try to control the natural world.

Trungpa Rinpoche goes on to offer some examples: "Push-button elevators, pre-packaged meat, air conditioning, flush toilets, private funerals, retirement programs, mass production, weather satellites, bulldozers, fluorescent lighting, nine-to-five jobs, television—all are attempts to create a manageable, safe, predictable, pleasurable world." Again: it isn't that there's a problem with some of the civilized comforts we've created (although sustainability is an increasingly urgent question). His emphasis is on "the neurotic preoccupation that drives us to create them, to try to control nature." The "nature" that is closest to us is, of course, our own bodies. All of our efforts to completely control our bodies—through physical fitness, biomedicine, cosmetic surgery—are signs of this basic anxiety about physical form.

The good news is that it's possible to enjoy our bodies and the physical world without the grasping and fixation that often imprison us in worry and anxiety. In fact, we could enjoy and take much better care of the natural world of form and bodies without this fear-based distorting lens. When we are afraid of something, it's difficult to see it clearly. Under the influence of materialism, our whole relationship to form is founded on panic, as though we are constantly approaching the physical world and our bodies with a single, anxious question: "Are you for me or against me?" What kind of friendship is that?

The Lord of Speech

Similarly, the Lord of Speech doesn't mean the ideas and categories that we all use to make sense of our lives, the "speech" that we use to communicate. Again, what's meant is the neurotic "use of concepts as filters to screen us from a direct perception of what is," as Trungpa Rinpoche wrote. We use sets of ideas, systems of ideology, to reinforce a sense of solid, personal identity. When I first read these teachings, I was struck that Trungpa Rinpoche specifically mentions "nationalism, Christianity, Buddhism." Now we should continue by adding our favorite belief systems to the list, all the ideas we cling to.

This includes fixed ideas from psychology about who we really are and the real causes for that. We repeat these stories from the psychotherapeutic realm to ourselves again and again, taking these concepts about childhood experience in our families of origin more and more seriously: "I am this kind of person with this kind of problem because of what my parents did or did not do." What was once a fresh and living insight becomes congealed theory, lifeless and dry.

We also solidify ideas from the political realm about the solution to local and global challenges, about who's the real threat and who will actually help us. Examining this kind of materialism means looking at the tight grip we maintain on all our favorite theories: individualism, socialism, shamanism, "technologism." The result of this fixation? "I'm this kind of person! I hate those on the other side with their stupid, evil ideas." The inner sense of something lacking is replaced by the solid walls of territory: "Don't even mention those ideas in my house! How could I be friends with someone who thinks that?"

The Lord of Mind

The Lord of Mind is a way of describing the tendency to hold on to special, higher, or altered states of consciousness as a means of proving one's self-worth. Never mind things—I have enough of those, or even ideas—what I really want to get is enlightenment, a more compassionate heart, awakening. "Drugs, yoga, prayer, meditation, trances, various psychotherapies—all can be used in this way, " as Trungpa Rinpoche wrote.

Why are they called the three "lords"? It's an image for the rulers of the kingdoms of materialism. Sometimes they're also called the three "barbarian kings." The main point is: as long as we live our lives under their sway, there can be no peace. They constantly promote warfare, aggression, spiritual and psychological imprisonment. Walking the spiritual path is a way to free ourselves and others from their corrupt and degrading rulership.

So the nightmare of materialism does have to do with consumerism. How much of what we shop for is a matter of actual need? How much are we moved to buy and acquire more things in a desperate attempt to bring more solidity to our sense of self, to try to fill an inner emptiness? Consumerism is a spiritual issue.

When we turn to spiritual shopping, we often find ourselves working overtime under all three lords, not only the Lord of Mind: "Retreat to nature, isolation, simple, quiet, high people—all can be ways of shielding oneself from irritation, all can be expressions of the Lord of Form," says Trungpa Rinpoche. "In following a spiritual path we may substitute a new religious ideology for our former beliefs, but continue to use it in the old neurotic way . . . to maintain our ego." In our twenty-first century age of terror, the spiritual supermarket is growing explosively.

Here's the crucial connection: consumerism is based on that same sense of basic lack. The ads never say, "You're basically good just as you are—and therefore you should buy this." Usually the pitch is aimed at any underlying sense of insecurity or inadequacy, with a strongly implied hook: "If you buy this car or wine or cosmetic or watch or service, then people will love you." Implied: without this thing, if you don't manage to acquire it, you will be a miserable loser bereft of human companionship for the remainder of your sad, lonely days. If, on the other hand, you buy this particular brand of deodorant, it will give you the body and mind you desire, the body and mind that will be eternally desirable and loved by others. All these sales pitches are based on devaluing what we are. Whatever already is—even the product we bought last year—is so much less than what we could have, what we could be, with this shiny, new purchase.

Then there are the ads that appeal to a sense of being slightly better: if you're more intelligent, you'll drive this kind of car. The message in this case is not so much that you're "one down" as it is that we'll help you be "one up"—that is, you already are "one up," and you deserve the things that show it. There are many variations on the theme, and the game of one-upmanship is an endless pursuit. It can even be played in the spiritual realm: "My practice, teacher, and lineage are superior to yours. We've got much more egoless-ness!" The main factor in all these examples is the underlying nightmarish delusion that there is something basically wrong with us, that we need an add-on, an improvement, a fix-it job for our body, emotions, and mind. When we believe the nightmare of materialism, we disrespect ourselves and others, the world around us, in an endless search for more security, more things, an endless quest for more, more, more.

IS THERE ANY OTHER WAY?

I love discussing these issues with gatherings of meditators. Recently, someone told of a statement she'd read by an anticonsumerist activist: "Most people work forty-plus hours a week at jobs they don't like to buy things they don't need." In moments of despair we may wonder, "Isn't this just the way things are? If everybody's doing it, is there any other way?"

Meditation is a way of awakening from the nightmare of materialism. Just bringing mindfulness and awareness to our ingrained habitual patterns of grasping interrupts some of the automatic sleepwalking: "Suddenly I woke up and found myself at the cash register, a credit card in each hand, in yet another shopping mall."

The nightmare quality is the recurrent bad dream that we're never enough, others are never as they should be, and the world is sadly lacking. Mindfulness-awareness meditation allows us to compare this prevalent idea, this thought, with how we actually are in this moment: it allows us to see what's actually going on, as opposed to the voices in our head about what's true. This is a small step toward dismantling the machinery of the nightmare, of awakening to its delusion, of seeing the fullness of what actually is: our bodies and the body of the world around us.

The atmosphere surrounding meditation is basically warm and welcoming. We are cultivating appreciation, friendliness, a sense of gratitude for what we already have and are. This undercuts the speed and restlessness of materialism of all sorts. We are training ourselves in appreciation of basic nature. The thoughts that arise, the lively emotions at play, the sensations of our body are all expressions of this original nature of goodness. Mindfulness includes all aspects of our being as part of our fundamental richness, the sacredness of life and the world.

NATURAL MEDITATION

The emphasis throughout this book is on meditation's naturalness. Viewing training as an expression of our basic nature is an antidote to approaching meditation as just more spiritual materialism. In chapter one, we encountered the declaration of a famous Tibetan meditation master: "the ultimate materialism is believing that one has to manufacture buddha-nature." When we approach any spiritual practice—mindfulness, chanting, zazen, visualization, or reciting mantras—from the point of view of *producing* goodness, of getting something we don't have, we've missed the point. We talked in an earlier chapter about how Suzuki Roshi stressed the importance of practicing meditation with "no gaining idea." That's saying the same thing as appreciating the richness of what already is.

THE CULTURE OF FAKING IT

These days there's a lot of attention being placed on global warming, so finding ways of decreasing some of the unhealthy effects of our society's runaway materialism seems more important than ever. Sometimes humanity seems like an addicted ego run wild, pursuing its pleasure even to the point of destroying life on the planet. Trungpa Rinpoche described the culture of materialism as "the setting-sun world"—a phrase that seems more apt than ever.

Meanwhile, since getting something or someone from outside to validate us becomes so important in life under this reign of materialism, the temptation is to adopt what some psychologists call a "false-self system." "Faking it" is a reasonable strategy, at least on the face of it. There's a feeling of something missing—or worse—in here, so I need to hide that and present a "full" fake version of myself, so others, out there, will like me and allow me to get what I want.

This false self can be a "smiley face" version—if that's what we think will gain us emotional approval. Or we may pretend to be tough and hard and unforgiving, even when we actually feel some underlying tenderness. It's as though we move through the world holding up a giant, hollow mask for others to see and approve of and praise. Of course if this mask does win approval—such a good, kind, brave, intelligent person!—this only reinforces the inner sense of emptiness, since, as we inwardly know only too well, the outer approval, affection, and love we're receiving are actually for the false self. ("I doubt that anyone would love me, if they really knew what I'm actually like inside.") Does this suggest a reason for the hollow, brittle self-esteem of so many contemporary celebrities?

These rewards for the false self in turn strengthen the grip of the sense of inner lack—and so the temptation to fake it increases. These personal patterns have a ripple effect; individuals relating to themselves and others on this basis make up an alienated society, groups of masks talking to masks. The result is a cultural matrix that rewards deception and suspects any genuineness as just another manipulative strategy. Trust seems naive if not impossible in this hall of mirrors. Amassing power comes from perfecting the presentation of lies. As Rinpoche remarks: "Deception is the magic of the setting sun."

Here are three comments from recent conversations on meditation and the culture of faking it:

Question: Sure I admit to playing the game sometimes. I can remember being out on a first date and deliberately hiding any points of difference with my potential "significant other." The sad thing is, sometimes years later, these habits of pretending—of repressing what I'm actually like—set in, and this becomes the entire basis of the relationship. And then I begin to wonder: what kind of intimacy is this?

Q: Yeah—it's like the first day at a new job. You want to make a good impression. (My mother always warned me that first impressions count for a lot.) But here it is years later and I'm still filling any space during our coffee breaks with a funny story or a stupid joke I heard somewhere. It's still a fast-break game of impression management. The thing is, I would actually like some genuine friendships with my coworkers.

Q: And then there's the whole business of gender roles. Should I pretend to be more caring when that's seen as appropriately "feminine"? What if I don't feel very caring at that moment? I can really see how gender roles and expectations get in the way of genuine relating. I see guys trying to show that they're both sensitive and "manly," a guy's guy. What if real connections happen when we're not trying to prove anything to anyone?

A common thread of insight emerges in these comments: we both want and fear real intimacy based on genuineness. In explaining our indentured service to the three lords, Trungpa Rinpoche notes that we often use forms, speech, and states of mind to shield ourselves from "raw, rugged reality." Listening to these comments, contemplating them, I was struck by our basic human vulnerability. Our hearts are affected by those we love and care for around us. This basic openness is then covered over in various ways—out of fear, out of the nightmarish delusion of inner scarcity. But the fundamental longing is to connect. We want to be with others in meaningful, genuinely supportive ways. Our dialogues have led us to a concluding consideration: natural wakefulness as the basis for genuine communities.

12 Awakening Communities of Courage

The Good Ground of Awakened Heart

THE SPIRITUAL PATH presented here passes over steep mountains, through boring meadows, and into lush valleys —all part of a meditator's journey. From the beginning, a key skillful means on this unfolding path is appreciating the good ground of our journey. We call this ground "basic goodness," the inherently compassionate wakefulness of our original nature. Suzuki Roshi reminds us that buddha-nature "is just another name for human nature." This fundamental wakefulness—the essence of all the awakened ones—may be uncovered and strengthened in individual meditation practice, but it flowers fully and beautifully in the form of sane and compassionate human communities.

Our longing for genuine community reflects the very nature of being human. We are unique as a species in the length of time our newborns require before even attempting self-sufficiency. Other species—from ducks to bears—pass into fully functioning maturity much more quickly.

We humans, on the other hand, depend on other human beings for years to lead us into the human family, to show us the original way, the way of being human. Feral children—"wild children" who have been stolen away from humans by other animals—like the boy depicted in François Truffaut's movie *L'Enfant Sauvage (The Wild Child)*—usually have great difficulty, upon reentering the human community, learning language or walking upright. Being around other human beings, hearing their voices speaking or laughing, seeing their loving, round faces beaming down at us, has an actual physiological effect on the development and maturation of our nervous systems. It's a simple, scientific fact: being with other humans is an absolute necessity for becoming fully human.

So, our basic human-heartedness exists as both inborn potential (our nature as human beings) and a quality in need of careful training through gentle cultivation. Suzuki Roshi used to joke, looking out at his students: "You're perfect as you are—and you could use some improvement." In the context of becoming human, this social training is called "acculturation"—a way of growing, developing, ripening our inner potential. Someone shows us how to tie our shoes, how to tell a joke, how to say "I'm sorry" and mean it. We all receive a basic cultural transmission, call it the universally required course in Being Human 101: "This is how we mourn our dead; this is how to give a good-night kiss; this is how we say 'good morning' (*buenos días, ohayo gozaimasu, bonjour*)." Someone trains us: this is how you take a birthday present to your good friend's birthday party. This is how to blow out the candles. This is how to help clean up afterward. All of these actions are learned—not genetically encoded—from other humans who pass on what was passed on to them: a favorite family recipe for making delicious gravy or piquant salsa; a love of trees or jazz or the ocean; a passion for movies, sports, social justice. This is how you make chords on a guitar, this is how you sing a song, this is how you steal second base, this is how you write your name in the sand, and this is how we dance. These were our first mentors—the ones who introduced us to the basic ways of being human. They transmitted to us the art of being human.

So, once again, our path of awakening blends training and nature. As we saw with meditation: without seeds, all the exertion in the world will be fruitless. Great-grandfather Tilopa transmitted the understanding that diligently pressing sand with mortar and pestle will never yield sesame oil— no matter how hard or how long we press. On the other hand, without some effort, even the best seeds will continue to lie dormant and unexpressed. This chapter explores this nature of loving-kindness, the many ways it's covered over, and the path to uncovering this vulnerability as true strength. We are looking at living with others as both a direct *path* of awakening the heart and the desired collective *fruition*: a compassionate way of living together, making enlightened culture.

This is particularly worth contemplating in our time of war, increasing violence, and domestic abuse. One of the greatest teachers of fundamental human-heartedness lived in ancient China. Confucius, known as "Master K'ung," lived in a time scholars call the Warring States period, teaching a contemplative path for reconnecting with our human-heartedness—and the essential humanity of even our most threatening enemies. He taught a way of peace that emphasized cultivating human kindness and mutual respect. Everyone—even those who would harm us—had a mother, someone who cared for them, someone they cared for and loved. As is said in the teachings of Mahayana Buddhism, even the fiercest animals have some tenderness toward their young. Even those who resort to violence have a basic gentleness that has been thickly crusted over with habits of greed and aggression. Insight shows us that the arrogant and selfish among us suffer from layer upon layer of confusion. Their confused actions proceed from a basic ignorance, a fundamental misrecognition, of the nature of human vulnerability. In our nature, we are beings of empathy and tenderness. We feel—and respond to—the sadness and joy of others. We resonate—just as one string on a guitar vibrates when another nearby is plucked. But, as the slaughterhouse of human history abundantly shows, when we lose touch with this basic human-heartedness, we are capable of immense destructiveness.

Contemplating, touching our fundamental human-heartedness, is then one of the best ways of developing it, strengthening it, and eventually gaining complete confidence in this original nature of goodness. We can contemplate a simple phrase such as "May all beings be happy" to quicken the inward impulse toward kind speech and action. The more we ingrain such an impulse, the more our first response upon meeting others (whether at home or at work) will be friendliness, loving-kindness.

As we considered in chapter 1 of this book: if such an impulse were not in fact deeply native to human nature (part of what Trungpa Rinpoche called our "enlightened genes"), all of us would stay as far as possible from any form of compassionate training. When I lived in northern California, we would burn citronella-scented candles on the patio in the evenings as an insect repellent. If our natures were not fundamentally already tending toward good-heartedness, we all would avoid the very words "compassion" or "love" in a similar way, as pungent repellents: "Sorry—that kindness stuff is definitely not for me. No, no! I'm only interested in training to become more selfish, to manipulate the world better so that I am always one-up! Never mind anybody else—who cares about them?"

As Traleg Kyabgon points out in his inspiring teachings on cultivating awakened heart, we have true insight when we see that such selfishness actually weakens us, that an open mind and caring heart are truly strengthening, enriching our lives and those of others.

So—our basic longing to be in community is the key ingredient here. Walking the path of natural wakefulness means recognizing that the circle of our concern reaches out well beyond our own body and mind to our family, friends, neighbors, coworkers, colleagues, customers, clients, patients, classmates, band members, teams, online correspondents, congregations, and spiritual communities as well as to the other citizens of our country and to the other residents of our continent and planet. Welcome to the family of great compassion.

THE PATH OF COMPASSIONATE BRAVERY

Cultivating the heart of compassion involves engaging both our attitude and our actions. We begin by strengthening our mental attitude, the courage to care for others. If we want to travel to India, first we think about the reasons for going, our motivation. Is it really worth it? How much will it cost, and how difficult will it be to go right now? What will be the benefit to ourselves and others? The great Indian Mahayana master Shantideva (Divine Peace) wrote that the hardships of the path of awakening seem tiny when compared to the immense benefit that comes from rousing compassion. The first step is stabilizing the wish, the aspiration, the desire to wake up completely as a being of power and tenderness. But strengthening our intention to be of benefit, to help others materially, psychologically, and spiritually, is only the preliminary to actually doing so. At a certain point the adage is relevant: "Don't just sit there, do something!" Let's walk

now through some ways of cultivating an enlightened attitude and then move on to the challenge of carrying out this
intention in the rest of our life.

CONTEMPLATING COMPASSION

The centuries-old tradition of contemplative Mahayana is
both profound and vast—containing diverse, skillful ways
of awakening the heart. There is, for example, the contemplative practice of *tonglen*, "sending and taking," radiating
goodness and taking on the suffering of others. This widely
taught practice is itself one part of a whole set of penetrat-
ingly practical teachings called, in Tibetan, *lojong*—literally,
"training the mind."

The specific instructions for contemplative meditation
presented here are based on the methods passed on by
my teacher Sakyong Mipham. This kind of contemplation
involves placing the attention on a thought or intention in
the form of words, a phrase or slogan. As is traditional, we
can contemplate limitless compassion using the phrase "May
all beings be free from suffering." When the mind wanders,
we return to these words as a touchstone, and we use these
words to plumb the deeper meaning, the experiential sense,
of compassion.

How so? It's as though we wanted to dive down to the
bottom of a clear, blue lake; we might hold on to a heavy
stone as it sinks, to carry us along to the depths. In this
case, these words ("May all beings be free from suffering")
are our stone—and we repeat them silently, thinking about
their meaning. As we say the phrase, we encourage images of
various kinds of suffering to play across the mind—different
forms of physical suffering, mental anguish, psychological
anxiety, the root suffering of spiritual fixation. All of these
touch our heart and kindle the warmth of compassion. As

images of suffering arise, we arouse and strengthen the wish for the liberation of all beings drowning in the ocean of suffering. As the feeling of compassion—here defined as the wish that beings not suffer—develops, we can let the words go and simply rest in this strong aspiration itself. When, as usually happens, the mind begins to wander ("Did I answer that e-mail from Ted?"), we then return to the phrase as our contemplative object and proceed through once again, deepening and stabilizing our compassionate resolve to free beings from suffering as we go.

Many of the obstacles in this practice will be familiar from our mindfulness meditation. The mind will wander into playgrounds of distraction ("What was that new DVD I meant to rent?") and even onto topics of other worthwhile labors ("I really should call her back soon about that scheduling glitch."). Our previous practice of taming the mind will be helpful in this further training of the mind and heart in a more expansive attitude. We are also continuing to tame the mind by practicing contemplation: "Stay, stay, reflect on the meaning of the words [followed by a period of wandering]; come back again; stay . . . , stay . . . ," and so forth. For an experienced meditator, this contemplative journey is both familiar terrain and new ground: now we're skillfully using our *thoughts* and *imagination* as part of the awakening process.

We may also notice some of the same habitual patterns and emotional conflicts rearing their heads during contemplation as during mindfulness-awareness practice. If jealousy is our favorite tendency, we may find ourselves somewhat reluctant, resistant even, to the mere thought of compassion, finally stopping short of wholeheartedly wishing that Jay not suffer—since, after all, he's had it so easy he deserves a few rocks in his road, doesn't he? Clearly, this is an obstacle to developing complete compassion. If we envy Pam her recent promotion at work ("Why didn't I get that job?"), we may find our contemplation drifting off at just the moment we remember her face. Perhaps, even if we've had plenty of sleep and are well-rested, we often find ourselves nodding off during our sessions of contemplative practice. Once again, the general guidelines of tightening and loosening apply—along with sharpening the eye of insight into recurrent habitual patterns and reactive emotional ruts.

The point here is that defensiveness and revenge scenarios and elaborate fantasies of getting this pleasure followed by that one—the same patterns of reactivity we noticed in our mindfulness practice—may show up during contemplation as well. Indeed, since these contemplations circle around our relationships to others, various conflicting emotions—including a sense of despair and discouragement about the whole process—may arise.

Often, in group retreats, someone will point out that it's not really very likely that all beings will be happy—or free from suffering—any time soon: "So what's the point of doing this?" This contemplation is not about the likelihood of beings enjoying happiness or the root of happiness by, say, next Thursday. Nor is it even a contemplation of "the best practices" for bringing this devoutly-to-be-desired result about as soon as possible. The contemplation is, so to speak, upstream from such pragmatic considerations and predictions. (At another time, it would certainly be worthwhile to think through the effectiveness of various approaches to helping; that would be a different contemplative inquiry into skillful means, *upaya*.) But this contemplation's primary purpose is to strengthen our wish for the well-being of others. We are, for the moment, working with stabilizing our aspiration: "May the suffering of all beings be alleviated; may they be liberated from the prison of confusion."

Why do this? Because, initially at least, even our wishing is unstable, wishy-washy. Some days we arise genuinely wishing others well—and that simple good-heartedness may last most of a workday. Other days we find ourselves suspicious and short-tempered, mean-spirited and ungenerous in thought, speech, and action with even our favorite friends at work. If we already abide in limitless loving-kindness and compassion throughout every day, then we do not need to practice these contemplations. Since, for most of us, that is not the case, Dr. Buddha's wise prescription still applies: Take the medicine of practice regularly, mornings and evenings, as needed.

Although this practice of cultivating loving-kindness (*metta, maitri*) and compassion (*karuna*) is part of a traditional sequence contemplating "the four limitless ones," many of us discover along the way the apparent limits of our heart's radiance. For now, I have some difficulty wishing my least favorite politicians happiness. As always, it's important to be honest—and not become angry with ourselves that we have not yet realized unlimited friendliness. We start where we are, as a famous American Buddhist nun reminds us, and we make friends with ourselves as we are, as the basis for extending further kindness to others.

Contemplative practice holds up a bright, clear mirror, precisely reflecting our state of mind and heart. It can be sobering to glimpse how deep-rooted our selfish tendencies really are. As Sakyong Mipham says: "Many of us are slaves to our minds. Our own mind is our worst enemy. We try to focus, and our mind wanders off. We try to keep stress at bay, but anxiety keeps us awake at night. We try to be good to the people we love, but then we forget and put ourselves first." This "forgetful" selfishness is not really an accident; we're discovering deeply ingrained habits of the heart. Recognizing the force of ego-driven momentum is a first step in replacing these tendencies with harmonious habits more aligned with our compassionate nature.

THE TRULY ADVANCED PRACTICE
OF EVERYDAY LIFE

*The everyday practice is simply to develop a complete
acceptance and openness to all situations and emotions.*
—Trungpa Rinpoche

After rousing a mind and heart that care for others, we enter
into daily life carrying that motivation, the strong wish to be
of benefit to others. Eventually, like being swept along by
a powerful rushing river, this stream carries us into action:
giving material support and encouragement, being patient,
extending ourselves to lighten someone's burden—and then
extending ourselves again. For most of us, there is no fore-
seeable shortage of opportunities to work with the anguish,
suffering, and despair around us.

The skillful approach is to use the daily challenges of family and work relationships as ways of awakening the heart,
steps on the path of compassion. From the smallest irritations in a home ("Dammit, who left the refrigerator door
open again?") to the increase of rude behavior in public spaces
(road rage at being cut off in traffic), all our interactions with
others involve communicating. The way we drive our morning
commute or ride our bicycle, the way we speak, the way we
hand someone a file folder—either we're expressing mindlessness, carelessness, and speed or mindful consideration and
respect for others.

Human beings are sensitive to the actions of those around
them. Some workplaces are filled with backbiting and snide
remarks, undercurrents of barely concealed resentment and
jealousy. We dread returning to such environments not because
of the workload (which often looms fearfully larger than it
really is in such surroundings) but because we hate the atmosphere that radiates discouragement and quiet desperation.

Walking the path of awakening the heart means stepping into any environment with the strong motivation of care and appreciation. If we are in touch with our own heart, our way of being is naturally encouraging to others, supporting their bravery and genuineness. The French word *coeur* means "heart." It's the source of the English word "courage." The Tibetan teacher Patrul Rinpoche is said to have greeted people not by asking, "How have you been?" but instead, "Has your heart been kind?" A worthwhile contemplation at the end of each day would be to think back over our activities and whether what we did or said was discouraging or encouraging for those around us. This self-reflection is not a matter of seeking praise or blame, a gold star or an internal reprimand. The point is daily mindfulness of our state of being and its expression. We are not only born into certain situations; we are making the environments we live and work in. As the title of a book of poems has it: "The life you ordered has arrived." This daily contemplation is simply asking ourselves: what kind of life are we ordering and making for ourselves and others?

So now we've moved from strengthening our skillfulness in compassionate wishing to considering our actual "entering in" to social engagement; the question becomes: what are we doing and how are we doing it? Notice however that—in an argument at work about meeting the deadline for a project, or a family debate about increasing monthly expenses—we're still receiving valuable feedback about our state of mind: are we being prideful, lording it over the others? No wonder they have such resistance to our newest brilliant idea! Are we being cowardly and weak—pretending to "go along just to get along," all the while storing up resentment that will eventually spill out in some sharply stinging remark? This too is mindfulness of mind—not just sitting still in a chair or on a cushion. The very moment of impatience—"Why is he taking so long to say he's sorry?"—is the ideal opportunity for practicing patience, seeing the present moment beyond hope or fear.

Challenges abound in living out our compassionate intention: that's why it's called the path of bravery. We discover that it is much easier to calmly abide in a quiet meditation hall than in crowded and speedy offices, on busy city streets, along subways and freeways. "Entering in" means that we begin to learn skillfulness. It's not enough just to wish for other's well-being. We learn from our life that this action, that word, was simply not helpful. This isn't a mysterious process; people will say to us: "All right, already. Stop trying to be so helpful; it's only making me feel worse!" This is clear feedback. We can then adjust our course accordingly: not every problem needs to be fixed; sometimes just being quietly present is more than enough. At other times we need to actively lean in—with food, money, goods, helping someone get the services they and their children desperately need. It's not enough in such a moment just to do *tonglen.* ("Excuse me, I can see you're bleeding, but I need further meditation practice before I can really help.") The point of the *tonglen* practice is to prepare our motivation for awakened activity. When the moment that needs our attention arrives, hesitation would be violating our own commitment to wakeful service.

So we learn skillful means through a kind of on-the-job training. There is no other way. This is necessarily a trial-and-error process, a path in which we are willing to make mistakes and learn from them. We cannot develop compassionate skill by remaining in retreat or avoiding life's conflicts. We cannot learn "skill in means" by theorizing beforehand; that would be like trying to learn to dance the Argentine tango by sitting still, staring at a computer screen. If we want to learn to swim, at some point it's necessary to get in the water.

The turbulent ups and downs of life—including "work, sex, and money," as Trungpa Rinpoche phrased it—are true training grounds for bravery and warriorship. The challenges of our life are ideal situations for waking up and encouraging others; and we need to accept those challenges in this very life, not another idealized life of fantasy, but the life we have at this moment—in these relationships with these people, in this job, this neighborhood, this city, this country. In *Shambhala: The Sacred Path of the Warrior*, Trungpa Rinpoche expresses this unequivocally: "Abstract caring about others is not enough. The most practical and immediate way to begin sharing with others and working for their benefit is to work with your domestic situation and expand from there. So an important step in becoming a warrior is to become a family person, someone who respects his or her everyday domestic life and is committed to uplifting that situation."

THE NATURAL PATH OF AWAKENING THE HEART

We have been emphasizing the necessity of effort on the path of mindful social engagement. It takes discipline and exertion to notice our states of mind, extend ourselves to others, and stick with it. On the other hand, many avenues for uncovering and ripening goodness are built right into our lives already— more signs that the path of human-heartedness is entirely natural to us, perhaps even universal. It's a pervasive and powerful innate desire—to wake up into loving, courageous lives with others. In waking up and helping others, we are going with the grain of our nature.

Consider, for example, parenting as a path. It engages tenderness and love that seem spontaneously present, and it requires integrity and the ability to sound a caring but firm "no." Our love and care for our own parents develops compassionate qualities of the heart as well, maturing and ripening over time. Similarly, any art form that we engage encourages creative play with form, color, sound, physical movement—the celebration of the goodness of our senses and the phenomenal world. The healing arts follow similar lines of development; the martial arts are famous for "joining heaven and earth." Some days the exertion of our job feels uplifting, inspiring, as we delight in helping others—this is work as a spiritual practice. Being a good friend during times of grief—all of these are paths of the natural unfolding of the fullness of the human heart.

OBSTACLES TO BUILDING AWAKENED COMMUNITIES

So, then, if waking up for the benefit of others is such a strong, widely available, and enduring impulse—like a vast underground river that rises to the surface again and again—why do most of us find ourselves living in neighborhoods, communities, cities, countries that would at best be characterized as "unenlightened societies"? We turn our attention once again to obstacles, not in our individual bodies and minds, but in society at large. We need to contemplate collective obstacles to compassion, the almost demonic forces of materialistic outlook and practice, as the great destroyer of awakened community spirit.

In 2000, Harvard professor Robert Putnam published his monumental study of recent changes in the social life of the United States, *Bowling Alone: The Collapse and Revival of*

American Community. As Putnam explains: "The dominant theme is simple: For the first two-thirds of the twentieth century a powerful tide bore Americans into ever deeper engagement in the life of their communities, but a few decades ago—silently, without warning—that tide reversed and we were overtaken by a treacherous rip current. Without at first noticing, we have been pulled apart from one another and from our communities over the last third of the century." Putnam's study looks at the decline in "connections in the workplace" and in religious, civic, and political participation. He considers various reasons for these changes—and is suspicious of "single-cause" explanations: "It is tempting to assume that one big effect (like civic disengagement) has one big cause (like two-career families or materialism or TV), but that is usually a fallacy. A social trend as pervasive as the one we are investigating probably has multiple causes."

Among the range of possible causes, I focus here on the rising tide of materialism—not as a single-factor explanation, but as the most spiritually relevant contributor to the current illness of our social body. Recall that the core of the materialistic outlook is the sense of personal inadequacy, the feeling that "inside I'm just not enough." "In order to really love and respect myself, I need to pretend to be different than I am; I need to be and have more." This lack of self-respect, then, drives the increasingly desperate search to acquire and amass things from others, to try to compensate for that inner sense of emptiness, groundlessness, of never being good enough. We are repeatedly seduced by the three lords of materialism, as Trungpa Rinpoche taught, because they offer the deceptive promise of greater solidity. This is the spiritual background for understanding some of the trends and research findings Putnam cites: "When asked by Roper pollsters in 1975 to identify the elements of 'the good life,' 38 percent of all adults chose 'a lot of money,' and an identical

38 percent mentioned 'a job that contributes to the welfare of society.' The same question was then posed every three years, and by 1996 those who aspired to contribute to society had slipped to 32 percent, while those who aspired to a lot of money had leaped to 63 percent." We are turning away from each other out of fear. If the only promise of safety lies in gathering things, generosity to others seems a foolish luxury. The increasing seductiveness of attaining material security corresponds to the gradual erosion of collective well-being. This general cultural malaise has tangible, individual, personal effects. Putnam mentions public health epidemiologists' concern with generational increases in rates of suicide and depression; he quotes psychologist Martin Seligman: "The rate of depression over the last two generations has increased roughly tenfold."

The fear that underlies such collective sadness and hopelessness is directly related to a decline in the sense of trusting others. Putnam, again: "The fraction of high school seniors who agreed that 'most people can be trusted' was sliced exactly in half between the late boomers of 1976 (of whom 46 percent were trusting) and the late X'ers of 1995 (of whom only 23 percent were trusting." A painful irony of unintended consequences is at work here: the materialistic strategy for achieving "the good life" suggests that each of us focus narrowly on what we can acquire, leaving little time or energy for considering the well-being of others. If we all move in this direction, we actually do become less trustworthy— more self-centered and indifferent to the health of our communities. Materialism is a self-fulfilling prophecy: if we put all our trust in things, eventually only things will be trustworthy. Is that a sustainable world?

"It is in such times that we turn to spiritual teachings." Sakyong Mipham opens his guide to the practice of meditation, *Turning the Mind into an Ally,* by considering the unhappy character of the times we live in. All too often, the path to spiritual awakening is divorced from the actual political turbulence, the immense suffering, both locally and globally, of our historical era. One might think that the profound spiritual instructions carefully passed down to us were primarily to ease our anxiety about ourselves—the teachings as spiritual antidepressants. At the same time, some contemporary social and political movements, despite their worthy goals, seem cut off from the depth of inner experience, the dimension from which gentleness and celebration emerge. This book continues a tradition in which practicing awareness is a stepping-stone to radical social change, the kind of change necessary to truly protect the earth. Practicing the strength of mind of right meditation returns us to the courage of our own hearts, a place from which we can envision sane societies, communities of trust and compassion.

COMMUNITIES OF SANITY, GENEROSITY, AND CELEBRATION

This book ends with a vision of living within community as a powerful practice for uncovering and developing the innate goodness of a meditative path. Life in community is a training ground as well as the organic result of cultivating natural wakefulness. "Community" in the sense we are using it here includes many old and new forms of social gathering— neighborhood groups, environmental action alliances, PTA meetings, political caucuses, online virtual communities such as Facebook and MoveOn.org, the people we hang out with after class at our local yoga center. As well, there are the traditional spiritual families assembling around churches, synagogues, mosques, ashrams, and Buddhist sanghas.

I have been practicing in one such spiritual community for thirty-five years now. What I write here is based on that continually surprising voyage with others, a journey filled with discouragement and inspiration at my own and others' cowardice and bravery. It has been an experience of "sad joy." (The English word "sad" is related to "sated" or "satisfying." "Sad" originally meant the experience of a full heart.) Life in communities is filled with occasions of joy—the birth of children, graduations, weddings, birthday parties—which all seem inseparable from the sadnesses of what the Chinese call "tasting bitter," experiences of loss and grief at the dying of loved ones—friends from childhood and college, partners, revered teachers, old adversaries, and young companions on the path.

The communities we aspire to make together are marked by sanity, generosity, and celebration. Trungpa Rinpoche spoke often of cultivating "basic sanity." The English word "sane" is, of course, related to words for cleanliness: "sanitation," "sanitary." Communities of sanity support a basic self-reliance and tidiness; we clean up our own psychological confusion without leaning on anyone else to walk the path for us. This kind of group support is the ideal of the Buddhist vision of *sangha,* a truly "virtuous gathering in goodness." We are encouraged in the practice of mindful awareness to discover an unconditional, meditative well-being that allows us to stand upright in freedom. This is quite different from a community based on "idiot compassion," in which we are coddled and indulged and told that whatever we do or say is right. The social presence of such a community inspires us to walk mindfully, to live decently, with contentment and the joy of simplicity.

Communities of generosity are founded in a sense of basic richness, a wealth that cannot be acquired from outside. This is an expansion of the meditative discovery of well-being; it is the Mahayana Buddhist vision of unshakeable prosperity. Walking the path of bravery and compassion means overcoming the sense of scarcity—the nightmarish perception of a basic lack that drives so much grasping and aggression. There is a wise saying from a sutra: "Generosity is the virtue that produces peace." When giving is our first impulse, we invoke an atmosphere free from craving and cowardly, deceptive actions to fulfill that craving. Generosity encourages us in the bravery of being genuine—standing on our own feet while continuously offering to others. Like moonlight reflected in a hundred bowls of water at once, such giving is spontaneous and, as is said, offered without expecting anything in return.

Communities of celebration evoke and then bask in the joy of human togetherness. We share a common ground with our sisters and brothers, and that ground is a space for music and dance, for festivals and ritual gatherings. Communal feasts are the practice of great joy, looking up toward the space of heaven, down to the practicalities of earth, and horizontally at the family of basic goodness. Through the practice of meditative awareness in action, natural wakefulness blossoms as enlightened society.

ACKNOWLEDGMENTS

I THANK MY TEACHERS, Vidyadhara Trungpa Rinpoche and Sakyong Mipham Rinpoche, for opening the door to the treasury of oral instructions. May the dharma teachings of the Practice Lineage flourish.

I thank my acharya colleagues—sisters and brothers in the way of Shambhala—for challenging criticism and gentle encouragement. May our loyalty to the vision shine like the sun so the family of basic goodness may establish enlightened society.

I thank my companion, Arawana Hayashi, for inspiration. I wholeheartedly agree with C. Otto Scharmer (and many others) that, as an artist and teacher, she brilliantly illuminates the way of embodied presence.

Emily Bower of Shambhala Publications has been both insightful and extraordinarily patient in helping give birth to this book. Early versions were read and commented on by Judith L. Lief and Holland D. Hammond. Emily Bower noted my good fortune in having generous friends who are also professional editors. (Judy Lief, author of *Making Friends with Death,* edited several books for her teacher Chögyam

Trungpa Rinpoche. Holly Hammond is a former editor of the *Vajradhatu Sun* and *Yoga Journal*.) Although I gained new appreciation for the meaning of the phrase "ruthless compassion," I will always be grateful to these incisive readers.

I am also grateful for the kindness of early readings by Tulku Thondup Rinpoche, Traleg Kyabgon Rinpoche, Jack Kornfield, and John Welwood.

This book has been, as the old blues says, "a long time comin'," and the longer it has taken, the greater the number of people I need to thank. I taught the first versions of a Natural Wakefulness retreat while resident acharya at Karmê-Chöling meditation center in Vermont's Northeast Kingdom. Several month-long group meditation retreats, based on the same principles, followed at Shambhala Mountain Center in northern Colorado. I am grateful to the administrators, staff, and participants of all of these practice programs.

I thank my dharma sister Soto Zen priest Hilda Ryūmon Gutiérrez Baldoquín for her unwavering solidarity in advancing the liberatory potential of dharma. A bow to Acharya Pema Chödrön for the inspired suggestion that Hilda and I work together.

I am grateful to Carolyn Rose Gimian for the devotion and loyalty that produced *The Collected Works of Chögyam Trungpa*, without which (as Sherab Kohn put it) I would be deaf, dumb, and blind. I have received encouragement and support from Judith Simmer-Brown, William (Norbu) McKeever, Deborah Luepnitz, Adam S. Lobel, John Rockwell Jr., William and Pamela Bothwell, Polly Young-Eisendrath, T. V. H. and Margery Mayer, Mary S. Lang (for the photo), Chris Alicino (of www.ChristineAlicino.com), Barbara and Michael Smith, Ayla Teitelbaum and Kobun Kaluza, Father Alan Hartway (colleague and chair of the Department of Interdisciplinary Studies at Naropa University), Christopher Pleim, Larry Mermelstein and Scott Wellenbach of the

Nalanda Translation Committee, Thomas B. Coburn, Samuel Bercholz, Ethan Nichtern of the Interdependence Project, Juliet Wagner, Sensei Fleet Maull, Lin Waters, Daniel Hessey, John Weber of Naropa's Department of Religious Studies, my dharma brothers Cortez Rainey and Justin Miles, Noel Hayashi and Victor Gotesman of the Center for Creative Resources, Hazel Bercholz (for artful elegance), Emily Hilburn Sell, Ben Gleason, Marcia Cohen Fields, Peter Turner, Melvin McLeod, Jeff Waltcher, Brian Spielmann, Adana and Jonathan Barbieri, Eamon Killoran, Jesse Miller, Derek Kolleeny, Susan Dreier, and Ellias Lonsdale.

I thank the folks at Samadhi Cushions of Barnet, Vermont, for their generosity. I have been fortunate to join in the teaching work of the Shambhala Prison Community, led by William Karelis, and to practice meditation with the men incarcerated at the Donaldson Correctional Facility thanks to an invitation from Deborah Marshall. I thank the meditators and administrators at New York Insight Meditation Center; San Francisco Zen Center; Spirit Rock Meditation Center; the Shambhala centers of Berkeley, San Francisco, Los Angeles, Seattle, Bellingham, Portland (Oregon), Boston, New York, Montreal, Ottawa, the Kootenays (British Columbia), Vancouver, Burlington (Vermont), Pioneer Valley (Massachusetts), Saint Johnsbury (Vermont), Fort Collins and Boulder (Colorado), Marpa House (Boulder), Austin (Texas), and Birmingham (Alabama); and Sky Lake Lodge.

May all beings be liberated into natural wakefulness.

NOTES

Introduction

Dr. King called this the "dream of beloved community."

The nonviolent revolutionary social vision of the Reverend Dr. Martin Luther King Jr. is explored in depth in Kenneth L. Smith and Ira G. Zepp's *Search for the Beloved Community: The Thinking of Martin Luther King, Jr.* (Valley Forge, Pa.: Judson Press, 1974).

finding a "middle way"

This term has a rich variety of meanings in Buddhist tradition. Initially, in the First Turning of the Wheel Sutra, Shakyamuni proclaimed the discovery of a middle path (*madhyama pratipad*) between asceticism and indulgence. Later, Arya Nagarjuna taught a middle way (*madhyamaka*) between eternalism and nihilism.

nature and training

These two principles are derived from commentary in the Tibetan Buddhist tradition on the Sanskrit syllables *e* and *vam*. See volume 4, pages 122–23 of *The Collected Works of Chögyam Trungpa* (Boston: Shambhala, 2004).

there are also dialogues

Some readers have referred to this style of teaching (and learning) through call-and-response conversations of questions and answers as "Socratic." Other readers have noticed that the form of many Buddhist sutras is a dialogue of exchanges between voices of confusion and insight.

Chapter 1. Awakening to the Life of Reruns

One great Tibetan meditation teacher

This saying is attributed to Jamgön Kongtrul Lodro Thaye, also known as Jamgön Kongtrul the Great (1813–1899). See Chögyam Trungpa's *Training the Mind and Cultivating Loving-Kindness,* edited by Judith L. Lief (Boston: Shambhala, 1993), a book based on Kongtrul's commentary on the basic Kadampa text that Trungpa Rinpoche has translated as "The Root Text of the Seven Points of Training the Mind."

some questions contain their own answers

"So we don't have to search for the answers because the question contains the answer in it." Chögyam Trungpa, *Meditation in Action* (Boston: Shambhala, 1991), 29–30.

"It is wisdom which is seeking wisdom."

Shunryu Suzuki, *Zen Mind, Beginner's Mind* (Boston: Shambhala, 2006), 19.

original nature, fundamental wisdom, basic goodness

Original nature is the basis of Soto Zen meditation practice as taught in Shunryu Suzuki's *Zen Mind, Beginner's Mind,* 51. Basic goodness is the foundation of the Shambhala teachings as presented in Chögyam Trungpa's *Shambhala: The Sacred Path of the Warrior* (Boston: Shambhala, 1984), 42.

the ultimate materialism

Attributed to the third Karmapa, Rangjung Dorje, in Chögyam Trungpa and Herbert V. Guenther's *The Dawn of Tantra,* edited by Michael Sherap Kohn (Boston: Shambhala, 1975), 9.

As Tilopa explains
Tilopa (988–1069) was an enlightened Buddhist saint, one of the famous eighty-four *mahasiddhas.* A translation of his sesame seed *doha* (realization song) appears in the Nalanda Translation Committee's *The Rain of Wisdom: The Essence of the Ocean of True Meaning* (Boston: Shambhala, 1999), 126.

Chapter 2. Natural Training

"strong confidence in our original nature"
Shunryu Suzuki, *Zen Mind, Beginner's Mind* (Boston: Shambhala, 2006), 51.

"that which sees confusion is not itself confused"
This teaching is presented in the first chapter of Chögyam Trungpa's *Glimpses of Mahayana* (Halifax, Nova Scotia: Vajradhatu Publications, 2001), 1–8.

Chapter 3. Mindful Open Presence:
A Gentle Way of Training

what Harvard psychologist Ellen Langer calls "mindlessness"
Ellen S. Langer, *Mindfulness* (Cambridge, Mass: Da Capo Press, 1990).

Chapter 4. Home Ground:
Resting Attention in the Body

"matter reflects mind"
Chögyam Trungpa, *Cutting Through Spiritual Materialism* (Boston: Shambhala, 2002), 163.

a "Sitting Bull" quality
Chögyam Trungpa, *Cutting through Spiritual Materialism,* 105.

as Dzigar Kongtrül emphasizes
> Dzigar Kongtrül, *It's Up to You: The Practice of Self-Reflection on the Buddhist Path* (Boston: Shambhala, 2005).

"a quality of expansive awareness develops through mindfulness of body"
> Chögyam Trungpa, *The Heart of the Buddha*, edited by Judith L. Lief (Boston: Shambhala, 1991), 31.

"the ideal state of tranquility"
> Chögyam Trungpa, *Shambhala: The Sacred Path of the Warrior* (Boston: Shambhala, 1985), 41.

"synchronizing mind and body"
> Chögyam Trungpa, *Shambhala*, 51–52.

Chapter 5. Dancing Stillness: Helpful Hints on Mindfulness of Body Meditation

the four foundations of mindfulness
> An English translation of the Foundations of Mindfulness *sutta* appears in *The Middle Length Discourses of the Buddha: A Translation of the Majjhima Nikaya* (Teachings of the Buddha), translated by Bhikku Nanamoli and Bhikku Bodhi (Boston: Wisdom, 1995), 145. I am deeply indebted to Chögyam Trungpa's presentation of the tradition of oral instructions on these four in *The Heart of the Buddha*, edited by Judith L. Lief (Boston: Shambhala, 1991).

"eternal hitchhiker"
> Chögyam Trungpa, *The Heart of the Buddha*, 32.

"One tries to feel the breath"
> Chögyam Trungpa, *Meditation in Action* (Boston: Shambhala, 1996), 77.

"The human mind is by nature joyous"
> Sakyong Mipham, *Turning the Mind into an Ally* (New York: Riverhead Books, 2003), 25.

"From a Buddhist point of view, human beings . . . are inherently peaceful"
> Sakyong Mipham, *Turning the Mind into an Ally,* 25.

blindly wandering
> "The Song of Lodrö Thaye," in *The Rain of Wisdom,* translated by the Nalanda Translation Committee (Boston: Shambhala, 1999), 84.

"no gaining idea"
> Shunryu Suzuki, *Zen Mind, Beginner's Mind* (Boston: Shambhala, 2004), 60.

"journey without a goal"
> Chögyam Trungpa, *Journey without Goal: The Tantric Wisdom of the Buddha* (Boston: Shambhala, 2000).

"riding on oneself and playing a flute"
> Chögyam Trungpa, *1973 Seminary Talks* (Halifax, Nova Scotia: Vajradhatu Publications, 1974), 45.

a boa constrictor's approach
> Sakyong Mipham, oral teaching, various locations, 1999.

mind weeds
> Shunryu Suzuki, *Zen Mind, Beginner's Mind,* 36.

Maitreya asana
> Chögyam Trungpa, *Meditation in Action* (Boston: Shambhala, 1991), 76.

Chapter 6. Welcoming: The Feeling of Mindfulness

struggle and freedom
> Sally is referring to Chögyam Trungpa's *Cutting through Spiritual Materialism* (Boston: Shambhala, 2002).

"we may have a pleasant feeling"
> Thich Nhat Hanh, *Transformation in Healing: Sutra on the Four Establishments of Mindfulness* (Berkeley, Calif.: Parallax Press, 2006), 73.

rightdoing and wrongdoing
"Out Beyond Ideas," in *The Essential Rumi*, translated by Coleman Barks (San Francisco: HarperSanFrancisco, 2004), 16.

Chapter 7. *Fear and Abundance:* Conversations about Mindfulness of Feeling

"an old new world"
Chögyam Trungpa, 1973 *Seminary Talks* (Halifax, Nova Scotia: Vajradhatu Publications, 1974), 52.

"Let us do the touch and go"
Chögyam Trungpa, 1974 *Seminary Talks* (Halifax, Nova Scotia: Vajradhatu Publications, 1975), 13.

"The object of awareness is developed"
Chögyam Trungpa, *The Heart of the Buddha* (Boston: Shambhala, 1991), 33.

the novelist Toni Morrison
Jean Strouse's interview with Ms. Morrison appeared in the March 30, 1981, issue of *Newsweek*.

"The practice of the second foundation, mindfulness of feeling"
The Dzogchen Ponlop Rinpoche, "Tiny, Slippery Spot of Mind: The Four Foundations of Mindfulness in the Mahayana Tradition." *Buddhadharma* (Spring 2005), 25.

saying in the Shambhala tradition
The actual wording in *Shambhala: The Sacred Path of the Warrior* is "In order to experience fearlessness, it is necessary to experience fear." Chögyam Trungpa, *Shambhala: The Sacred Path of the Warrior* (Boston: Shambhala, 1985), 47.

"several stages in relating with the emotions"
Chögyam Trungpa, *The Myth of Freedom and the Way of Meditation* (Boston: Shambhala, 2002), 69.

"let be be finale of seem."
This is the seventh line of Wallace Stevens's poem "The Emperor of Ice Cream," first published in 1922. Thanks to Susan B. Dexter for introducing me to this poem.

Chapter 8. Finding Genuine Heart: Awareness of Mind's Flow

"The mindfulness of life"
Chögyam Trungpa, *The Heart of the Buddha,* edited by Judith L. Lief (Boston: Shambhala, 1991), 32.

"big mind"
Shunryu Suzuki, *Zen Mind, Beginner's Mind* (Boston: Shambhala, 2004), 35.

"Thoughts are a meditator's friend"
"Takpo Rinpoche, Gampopa (1079–1153)," translated by Herbert V. Guenther in *The Tantric View of Life* (Boston: Shambhala, 1976), 34.

Traleg Kyabgon . . . "mental states as the focus of meditation"
Traleg Kyabgon, *Mind at Ease: Self-Liberation through Mahamudra Meditation* (Boston: Shambhala, 2004), 150.

"the continuity of that mindfulness"
The Dzogchen Ponlop Rinpoche, "Tiny, Slippery Spot of Mind: The Four Foundations of Mindfulness in the Mahayana Tradition." *Buddhadharma* (Spring 2005).

"A quality of expansive awareness"
Chögyam Trungpa, *The Heart of the Buddha,* 31.

"reverse meditation"
Wangchuk Dorje, Karmapa IX (1556–1603), *The Transmission Pointing Out the Dharmakaya* (Halifax, Nova Scotia: Vajravairochana Translation Committee, 1991), 26.

Chapter 9. Seeing Beyond Hope and Fear: Conversations on Mindfulness of Mind

"good-enough life"
The idea of the "good-enough mother" was developed by the British psychoanalyst Donald Winnicott.

Indian meditation master Shantideva
Shantideva, an eighth-century Indian Mahayana Buddhist teacher, composed the classic guide to the path of compassion, the *Bodhicharyavatara*. The essential importance of paying attention to the mind is stressed in the first verse of the fifth chapter. See Shantideva, *The Way of the Bodhisattva*, translated by the Padmakara Translation Group (Boston: Shambhala, 2007).

Pema Chödrön mentions . . . pay attention to the tone of voice
Pema Chödrön, *The Wisdom of No Escape* (Boston: Shambhala, 2004), 18.

Tara Bennett-Goleman . . . the persistence of self-defeating mental "schemas"
Tara Bennett-Goleman, *Emotional Alchemy: How the Mind Can Heal the Heart* (New York: Three Rivers Press, 2002).

Ken McLeod and "reactive patterns"
Ken McLeod, *Wake Up to Your Life: Discovering the Buddhist Path of Attention* (New York: HarperCollins, 2001).

"six styles of imprisonment"
Chögyam Trungpa, *The Myth of Freedom and the Way of Meditation* (Boston: Shambhala, 2002), 17.

"the me plan"
Sakyong Mipham, *Ruling Your World: Ancient Strategies for Modern Life* (New York: Random House, 2005), 14.

"The world is ugly and the people are sad"
> This line is from Wallace Stevens's poem "Gubbinal," *Collected Poems* (New York: Knopf, 1954), 69.

"When you are completely identified with a pattern,"
> Ken McLeod, *Wake Up to Your Life,* 194–195.

like writing on water
> Longchenpa, *Four-Themed Precious Garland,* translated and edited by Alexander Berzin (Dharamsala: Library of Tibetan Works and Archives, 2001).

"It includes everything"
> Sakyong Mipham, *Turning the Mind into an Ally* (New York: Riverhead Books, 2003), xviii.

Chapter 10. Opening the Doors of Perception: Mindfulness of the Sense Fields

"sense perceptions are regarded as problematic"
> Chögyam Trungpa, *Shambhala: The Sacred Path of the Warrior* (Boston: Shambhala, 1985), 102.

"grasping and fixated"
> This is a direct translation of technical terms from Tibetan Buddhist tradition. The Nalanda Translators' glossary to *The Rain of Wisdom: The Essence of the Ocean of True Meaning* (Boston: Shambhala, 1999), 349, explains this pair as "the two processes that constitute the ego of self and the ego of dharmas. Objects are fixated on (Tib., *gzung wa'i yul*) as solid, independent existents, and the mind then grasps them (Tib. *dzin pa'i sems*)." These processes may be related to Acharya Pema Chödrön's discussion of *shenpa* in "How We Get Hooked and How We Get Unhooked," *Shambhala Sun,* March 2003.

"nothing special"
> Shunryu Suzuki, *Zen Mind, Beginner's Mind* (Boston: Shambhala, 2006), 46.

"Your sense faculties give you access"
Chögyam Trungpa, *Shambhala*, 102.

Chapter 11. Awakening from the Nightmare of Materialism

"getting and spending"
This is from the second line of that late chittamatrin William Wordsworth's poem "The World Is Too Much with Us" (1807): "The world is too much with us, late and soon, / Getting and spending, we lay waste our powers."

soft addictions
This concept is discussed, for example, in Judith Wright's *The Soft Addiction Solution* (New York: Tarcher, 2006).

"We must face the fact"
Chögyam Trungpa, *Shambhala: Sacred Path of the Warrior* (Boston: Shambhala, 1985), 48.

inner holes
A. H. Almaas, "The Theory of Holes," in his *Diamond Heart: Book One* (Boston: Shambhala, 2000), chapter 2.

The Three Lords of Materialism
All quotes in this passage are from Chögyam Trungpa, *Cutting Through Spiritual Materialism* (Boston: Shambhala, 2002), 3–11.

"setting-sun world"
Chögyam Trungpa, *Shambhala*, 57.

"false-self system"
This psychoanalytic notion was developed by Donald Winnicott and Ronald Laing. See chapter 6 of Laing's *Divided Self* (New York: Routledge, 1964).

"raw, rugged reality"
Chögyam Trungpa, *Cutting Through Spiritual Materialism*, 6.

Chapter 12. *Awakening Communities of Courage: The Good Ground of Awakened Heart*

buddha-nature
Shunryu Suzuki, *Zen Mind, Beginner's Mind* (Boston: Shambhala, 2004), 45.

"perfect as you are"
Quoted on the back cover of *To Shine One Corner of the World: Moments with Suzuki Roshi,* edited by David Chadwick (New York: Broadway Books, 2001). This book was republished by Shambhala Publications in 2007 with the title *Zen Is Right Here.*

cultivating awakened heart
Traleg Kyabgon, *The Practice of Lojong: Cultivating Compassion through Training the Mind* (Boston: Shambhala, 2007).

skillful means, upaya
The Nalanda Translation Committee's glossary defines *upaya* as an expression of compassion. "Generally, upaya conveys the sense that enlightened beings teach the dharma skillfully, taking into consideration the various needs, abilities, and shortcomings of their students." See *The Rain of Wisdom: The Essence of the Ocean of True Meaning* (Boston: Shambhala, 1999), 372.

"slaves to our minds"
Sakyong Mipham, *Turning the Mind into an Ally* (New York: Riverhead Books, 2003), 3.

"the everyday practice"
See more at Chögyam Trungpa with Rigdzin Shikpo (Michael Hookham), "The Way of Maha Ati," in volume 1 of *The Collected Works of Chögyam Trungpa,* edited by Carolyn Rose Gimian (Boston: Shambhala, 2004), 461–65.

"The life you ordered has arrived."
  Barbara Meier, *The Life You Ordered Has Arrived* (Berkeley: Parallax Press, 1988).

"Abstract caring about others"
  Chögyam Trungpa, *Shambhala*, 92.

"The dominant theme is simple"
  Robert Putnam, *Bowling Alone: The Collapse and Revival of American Community* (New York: Simon & Schuster, 2001), 27.

"It is tempting to assume"
  Putnam, *Bowling Alone*, 187–88.

"When asked by Roper pollsters"
  Putnam, *Bowling Alone*, 272–73.

"The fraction of high school seniors"
  Putnam, *Bowling Alone*, 260–61.

"It is in such times that we turn to spiritual teachings."
  Mipham, xvii.

RESOURCES

For information regarding meditation instruction or inquiries about a practice center near you, please contact one of the following:

Shambhala International
1084 Tower Road
Halifax, Nova Scotia
Canada B3H 2Y5
phone: (902) 425-4275, ext. 10
fax: (902) 423-2750
website: www.shambhala.org. This website contains information about the more than 100 centers affiliated with Shambhala.

Shambhala Europe
Annostrasse 27-33
D50678 Cologne
Germany
phone: 49-221-31024-10
website: www.shambhala-europe.org
e-mail: europe@shambhala.org

Karmê Chöling
369 Patneaude Lane
Barnet, Vermont 05821
phone: (802) 633-2384
fax: (802) 633-3012
e-mail: karmecholing@shambhala.org

Shambhala Mountain Center
4921 Country Road 68C
Red Feather Lakes, Colorado 80545
phone: (970) 881-2184
fax: (970) 881-2909
e-mail: info@shambhalamountain.org

Dechen Chöling
Mas Marvent
87700 St. Yrieix sous Aixe
France
phone: 33 (0) 5-55-03-55-52
fax: 33 (0) 5-55-03-91-74
e-mail: dechen-choling@shambhala.org

Dorje Denma Ling
2280 Balmoral Road
Tatamagouche, Nova Scotia
Canada B0K 1V0
phone: (902) 657-9085
e-mail: denma@shambhala.org

Gampo Abbey
Pleasant Bay, Nova Scotia
Canada B0E 2P0
phone (902) 224-2752
e-mail: office@gampoabbey.org

Meditation cushions and other supplies are available through:

Samadhi Cushions
30 Church Street
Barnet, Vermont 05821
phone (800) 331-7751
website: www.samadhistore.com
e-mail: info@samadhicushions.com

Naropa University is the only accredited, Buddhist-inspired university in North America. For more information, contact:

Naropa University
2130 Arapahoe Avenue
Boulder, Colorado 80302
phone (303) 444-0202
website: www.naropa.edu

Information about Sakyong Mipham Rinpoche, including his teaching schedule and a gallery of photographs, is available at his website:

www.mipham.com

Audio-and videotape recordings of talks and seminars by Sakyong Mipham Rinpoche are available from:

Kalapa Recordings
1084 Tower Road
Halifax, Nova Scotia
Canada B3H 2Y5
phone: (902) 420-1118, ext. 19
fax: (902) 423-2750
website: www.shambhalashop.com
e-mail: shop@shambhala.org

The *Shambhala Sun* is a bimonthly Buddhist magazine founded by the late Chögyam Trungpa Rinpoche and now directed by Sakyong Mipham Rinpoche. For a subscription or sample copy, contact:

Shambhala Sun
P.O. Box 3377
Champlain, New York 12919-9871
phone: (877) 786-1950
website: www.shambhalasun.com

Buddhadharma: The Practitioner's Quarterly is an in-depth, practice-oriented journal offering teachings from all Buddhist traditions. For a subscription or sample copy, contact:

Buddhadharma
P.O. Box 3377
Champlain, New York 12919-9871
phone: (877) 786-1950
website: www.thebuddhadharma.com

INDEX